A PICTORIAL HISTORY
OF THE
U.S. PRESIDENTS

A PICTORIAL HISTORY OF THE U.S. PRESIDENTS

Clare Gibson

GRAMERCY BOOKS
NEW YORK

To Robert, Anna, and Edward Malan.

This 2001 edition is published by Gramercy Books,™
a division of Random House Value Publishing, Inc.,
280 Park Avenue, New York, New York 10017,
by arrangement with PRC Publishing Ltd, London.

Gramercy Books™ and design are registered trademarks of
Random House Value Publishing, Inc.
Random House
New York • Toronto • London • Sydney • Auckland
http://www.randomhouse.com/

Printed and bound in China

A CIP catalogue record for this book is available
from the Library of Congress.

ISBN 0-517-16160-5

9 8 7 6 5 4 3 2 1

CONTENTS

The Presidential Oath
or Affirmation of Office

Before he [the president] enter on the Execution of his Office, he shall take the following Oath or Affirmation: "I do solemnly swear (or affirm) that I will faithfully execute the Office of President of the United States, and will to the best of my Ability, preserve, protect and defend the Constitution of the United States."

Section 1, Article II of the Constitution of the United States.

INTRODUCTION

Over two centuries have passed since the Constitution of the United States first gave executive power to the president. Since George Washington's election to the presidency in 1789 there have been 43 presidential incumbents: lawyers, soldiers, career politicians, rich men, poor men. All faced crises of one sort or another during their terms in office; some overcame them, others failed. Some presidents died in office—either as a result of the pressures of holding highest office, or by assassination. Certain incumbents, such as Washington, Lincoln, and Franklin Delano Roosevelt, manifested qualities of greatness, while the administrations of presidents such as Harding and Nixon were discredited. Despite the diverse personal attributes of those individuals who have been honored to serve as president, however, the presidential office itself remains a shining jewel in the crown of democracy, and one that has since been emulated by numerous nations.

Constitutional Government

In drafting the U.S. Constitution to provide for federal government in 1789, the Founding Fathers of the new nation of the United States had no precedent to follow. Having won their independence from a monarchical country in a bitter battle for democratic liberty there was no question of executive power being vested in an unelected, hereditary figurehead, such as the British king. The previous system of colonial governorship, as well as the Congress of the Confederation's committees and special agents, also appeared unsuitable. How best, then, to ensure that the United States would be governed both democratically and effectively? In formulating the Constitution the Founding Fathers drew heavily on the work of two great political thinkers—Locke and Montesquieu—who advocated a separation of governmental powers, and on the model of the New York governorship. On his election as the first president of the United States Washington observed: "I walk untrodden ground"; to him fell the awesome responsibility of translating the idealistic words of the Constitution into working practice, and to him must also be accorded the credit for doing so.

The solution that is enshrined in the Constitution represents a masterly allocation of governmental power, and includes a system of checks and balances designed to prevent abuse of that power. While, at the local level, the individual states enjoy a large measure of self-government by means of their own constitution, elected legislature, governor, and supreme court, at the national level power is divided between the judiciary, the legislature, and the executive branch—in effect, the president. Simultaneously head of state, of the armed forces, and of the civil service, as well as director of foreign affairs, the president selects his own cabinet, which must nevertheless

Former U.S. president Martin Van Buren and Charles Francis Adams run for president and vice president as leaders of the Free Soil Party, advocating "Free Soil—Free Labor—Free Speech."

measures (which are usually outlined in the annual State of the Union address). Depending upon the predominant political flavor of Congress, therefore, a president may find his recommendations either blocked or passed, which means that he must possess outstanding political and negotiating skills if he is to be successful. Proposed legislation must also be agreed by both houses, and conference committees will propose compromise legislation should deadlock occur. The president is entitled to veto legislation, but his veto can be overridden by a two-thirds majority in both chambers; along with the support of three-quarters of the state legislatures, a similar rule applies to any constitutional amendments. Today, the 100 senators (each state is represented by two) serve six-year terms, and elections are held every two years for a third of their number. The House of Representatives consists of 435 representatives, who are elected every two years from constituencies of approximately equal size. The judiciary, with the Supreme Court (comprising nine judges appointed by the president and approved by the Senate) at its head, ensures that the Constitution is correctly interpreted, in order to avoid any infringement of civil rights.

be approved by Congress. It is stipulated that the president, who is elected every four years by the Electoral College, must be a U.S. citizen of more than 35 years of age. By the terms of the 1951 Constitutional Amendment 22, the president may not serve more than two terms, and he or she cannot be removed from office, except by impeachment and conviction by Congress (in avoidance of which Nixon resigned).

The national legislature—Congress—consists of the Senate and the House of Representatives. Only the Senate can ratify foreign treaties and confirm federal appointments, and Congress must furthermore approve the president's policy

The Presidential Election

Traditionally, after a period of vigorous campaigning, the Democratic and Republican presidential candidates are nominated at their respective party conventions. A further period of campaigning follows, usually lasting from September to November (by the 20th Amendment of the Constitution of 1933 the president is elected on the Tuesday after the first Monday in November). The president is not elected directly by the people: in the national elections, citizens cast their votes for individuals drawn from a list of electors nominated by each party. Each state holds seats in the Electoral College, which alone is responsible for electing the president; the allocation of seats to states (of which there are 538) is roughly equivalent to that of the Senate and the House of Representatives, but no member of Congress or government official may participate. Electors usually (but not always) vote for the candidate with the greatest popular support. Votes for the president are counted in the respective states, and the winner is judged on a first-past-the-post basis, usually requiring a majority of 270 votes, but a president can be elected by a minority vote. A formal ballot takes place on the first Monday after the second Wednesday in December, when the state electors meet in each state, and the votes are then counted before Congress on January 6.

Inauguration

Between 1793 and 1933 the new president was inaugurated at noon on March 4. As a result of the 20th Amendment of the Constitution of 1933, however, since 1937 the Inauguration has taken place on January 20, thus shortening the period between the president's election and his induction into office. The president swears or affirms the oath of office, as laid down in Section 1, Article II, of the Constitution (see page 6); the vice president, too, is sworn in at the same ceremony. Those vice presidents who have become president as a result of the incumbent's death in office are sworn in immediately, and with little comparable ceremony. The Inauguration is traditionally held outside, and is followed by a parade and a celebratory ball.

The White House

With Inauguration Day over, the president sets to work to appoint his officials and to frame his policies. Since the days of John Adams (the United States' second president) he has done so at his official residence: the White House, at 1600 Pennsylvania Avenue, N.W., in Washington D.C.— a building nearly as old as the presidency itself.

The White House was originally planned by Washington, who also selected its site, and in 1792 an architectural competition was held to

A statue of Thomas Jefferson
in the rotunda of the Jefferson Hotel in Richmond, Virginia.

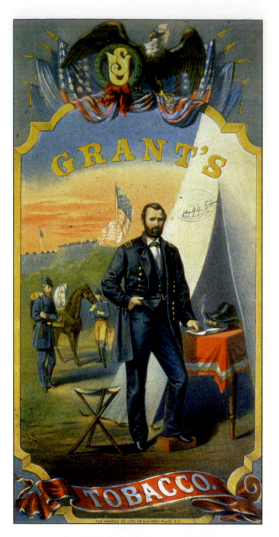

Grant's Cigar Card—January 1, 1874
A cigar card featuring the Union Army general and
18th president of the United States, Ulysses S. Grant.
Printed by The Graphic Co. Lith.

Adams took up residence. Disaster struck in 1814 during the war with Britain, when, after its remodeling by Benjamin H. Latrobe in 1806 under the instructions of Thomas Jefferson, British troops torched the building. It was rebuilt by James Hoban between 1815 and 1817, and it is said that its new, fresh, exterior earned it the appellation of the White House (although from 1818 to 1902 it was officially known as the Executive Mansion). The south portico was added in 1824, and the north in 1829.

Gas lighting was installed in 1848, central heating in 1853, and electricity in 1890. It was Chester A. Arthur who carried out the first major redecoration of the White House in 1881, when he commissioned Louis Tiffany to create a suitably magnificent interior, and his example was followed by Theodore Roosevelt, who added the west wing during his extensive remodeling program of 1902. As a result of the building work carried out by previous presidents, by the time of Truman's reelection in 1948 the White House was considered unsafe, and although the exterior was left intact the interior was effectively gutted and rebuilt over the next four years. To Jacqueline Kennedy goes the credit of turning the White House into an American showcase.

Today the 140-room White House stands in 18 acres of landscaped grounds. Located in the west wing are the president's Oval Office, the executive offices, the cabinet room, and the press room; other offices are situated in the east wing, which was built in 1942. On the first floor of the main building itself are the state rooms, and the presidential family occupies the second floor, while on the third floor can be found staff quarters, guest rooms, and a promenade.

select the best design for the projected presidential residence. The winner of the $500 prize was James Hoban, who proposed a neo-Palladian mansion of light-gray Virginia sandstone, with a rounded bay at the south front; the cornerstone was laid in the same year. By 1800 the mansion was deemed ready for occupation, and John

Hero's Welcome—April 23, 1789
Arrival of the first president of the U.S., George Washington, in New York to a hero's welcome.

As well as serving as the presidential office, as an appropriate place in which to receive foreign guests, and as a family home, this versatile building (whose running costs are shared by the president and Congress) has become a world-famous symbol of the dignity and power of both the president and the United States.

Conclusion

The lives of the distinguished line of American presidents are detailed in the following pages. Today, some of them are considered greater than others, but it should always be remembered that, in the words of President Eisenhower, which were quoted in 1962 by President Kennedy: "No easy problems ever come to the President of the United States. If they are easy to solve, somebody else has solved them." Throughout all the vicissitudes of the history of the United States, and despite the human shortcomings of its incumbents, the presidency itself has survived as an enduring testimony to the success of democratic government.

Clare Gibson

1.

GEORGE WASHINGTON (b.1732, d.1799)

Federalist. President 1789–1797

Vice president: John Adams

Termed the "Father of his country," it was largely due to George Washington's efforts that the New World colonies became an independent nation. As the first president of the United States he furthermore laid solid foundations for today's system of federal government.

Born in 1732 in Westmoreland County, Virginia, to a wealthy family, Washington was descended from an English immigrant. Having shown an early aptitude for surveying, in 1749 he was appointed surveyor of Culpeper County, and in 1752 he inherited the Mount Vernon estate.

Washington's distinguished military career began in 1753, when the governor of Virginia sent him to Fort Le Boeuf to reaffirm British claims in the face of French aggression. His daring led to a similar mission, during which, in 1754, a French detachment was wiped out, precipitating the French and Indian War. Washington was forced to surrender; undeterred, his subsequent bravery earned him the command of Virginia's troops. By the time that the war ended he had gained a dashing reputation, leadership experience, and a distrust of the British; he resigned his commission in 1758.

Washington was a member of the Virginia House of Burgesses from 1759 to 1774, during which period British legislation reinforced his belief that Britain intended to subject the American colonies to tyrannical rule. Elected to the first Continental Congress, he was instrumental in its adoption of the Fairfax Resolves, which created an autonomous government. By the time of the second Continental Congress of 1775 British troops were surrounded in Boston, leading to the establishment of the Continental Army, with Washington its commander-in-chief.

The conflict escalated; when George III branded Washington a traitor, this confirmed Washington's belief that the Union must become independent, and he was a crucial figure behind the Declaration of Independence of July 4, 1776. Washington was an outstanding military commander whose modern style of warfare confounded the British Army. Quickly recruiting and training his army, he was also responsible for the creation of an embryonic navy. His successes during the War of Independence included forcing the evacuation of British troops from Boston and the capture of Hessian mercenaries at Trenton in 1776; in 1777 he defeated Howe at Burgoyne, while his victory over Cornwallis at Yorktown effectively ended the war.

By the democratic organization of his army, and his refusal to indulge in political in-fighting, Washington had earned popular support and political respect. When the debts incurred during the war led to instability within the Union, the cool-headed, experienced Washington was an obvious choice as a leader to restore the equilibrium. Voted president of the Constitutional Convention in 1787 (which drafted the U.S. Constitution), his suggestion for a three-tiered government, in which power was divided between the executive branch (the president), the legislature, and the judiciary, was instituted.

After his unanimous election as the Union's first president, Washington was inaugurated in 1789. During his presidency he laid the foundations for political institutions which still survive. Balancing liberal and conservative tendencies, and displaying characteristic thoroughness and high standards, Washington demonstrated outstanding ability and integrity. He developed the executive cabinet, war, state, treasury, and postmaster-general departments, while his Federalist Program provided for the payment of revolutionary debts, currency reform, and the encouragement of domestic industry. Further achievements included the establishment of the federal court system. In his foreign policy, Washington proclaimed the United States' neutrality *vis-à-vis* Britain and France and secured trading rights and a new boundary on the 31st Parallel from Spain.

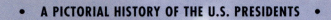

The American general and later the first president of the United States, George Washington on the battlefield.

Washington was reelected unanimously in 1792, but, in accordance with the Constitution that he had signed in 1787, and that he always upheld rigorously, decided not to seek a third term. He retired in 1797 to Mount Vernon, where he died in 1799. The words of Thomas Jefferson paid him fulsome tribute: "He was, indeed, in every sense of the word, a wise, a good, and a great man."

Before he was elected the U.S.A.'s first president, Washington served as the president of the Constitutional Convention, the body that drafted the U.S. Constitution. Article II of the Constitution laid down the terms and conditions for the election, powers, and functions of the president of the U.S.A.

Article II of the Constitution of the United States, 1787

"SECTION 1. The executive Power shall be vested in a President of the United States of America. He shall hold his Office during the Term of four Years, and, together with the Vice President, chosen for the same Term, be elected, as follows.

"Each State shall appoint, in such Manner as the Legislature thereof may direct, a Number of Electors, equal to the whole Number of Senators and Representatives to which the State may be entitled in the Congress: but no Senator or Representative, or Person holding an Office of Trust or Profit under the United States, shall be appointed an Elector.

"The Electors shall meet in their respective States, and vote by Ballot for two Persons, of whom one at least shall not be an Inhabitant of the same State with themselves. And they shall make a List of all the Persons voted for, and of the Number of Votes for each; which List they shall sign and certify, and transmit sealed to the Seat of the Government of the United States, directed to the President of the Senate. The President of the Senate shall, in the Presence of the Senate and House of Representatives, open all the Certificates, and the Votes shall then be counted. The Person having the greatest Number of Votes shall be the President, if such Number be a Majority of the whole Number of Electors appointed; and if there be more than one who have such Majority, and have an equal Number of Votes, then the House of Representatives shall immediately chuse by Ballot one of them for President; and if no Person have a Majority, then from the five highest on the List the said House shall in like Manner chuse the President. But in chusing the President, the Votes shall be taken by States, the Representation from each State having one Vote; a quorum for this Purpose shall consist of a Member or Members from two thirds of the States, and a Majority of all the States shall be necessary to a Choice. In every Case, after the Choice of the President, the Person having the greatest Number of Votes of the Electors shall be the Vice President. But if there should remain two or more who have equal Votes, the Senate shall chuse from them by Ballot the Vice President.

"The Congress may determine the Time of chusing the Electors, and the Day on which they shall give their Votes; which Day shall be the same throughout the United States.

"No Person except a natural born Citizen, or a Citizen of the United States, at the time of the Adoption of this Constitution, shall be eligible to the Office of President; neither shall any person be eligible to that Office who shall not have attained to the Age of thirty five Years, and been fourteen Years a Resident within the United States.

"In Case of the Removal of the President from Office, or his Death, Resignation, or Inability to discharge the Powers and Duties of the said Office, the Same shall devolve on the Vice President, and the Congress may by Law provide for the Case of Removal, Death, Resignation or Inability, both of the President and Vice President, declaring what Officer shall then act as President, and such Officer shall act accordingly, until the Disability be removed, or a President shall be elected.

"The President shall, at stated Times, receive for his Services, a Compensation, which shall neither be encreased nor diminished during the Period for which he shall have been elected, and he shall not receive within that period any other Emolument from the United States, or any of them.

"Before he enter on the Execution of his Office, he shall take the following Oath or Affirmation:- 'I do solemnly swear (or affirm) that I will faithfully execute the Office of President of the United States, and will to the best of my Ability, preserve, protect, and defend the Constitution of the United States.'

"SECTION 2. The President shall be Commander in Chief of the Army and Navy of the United States, and of

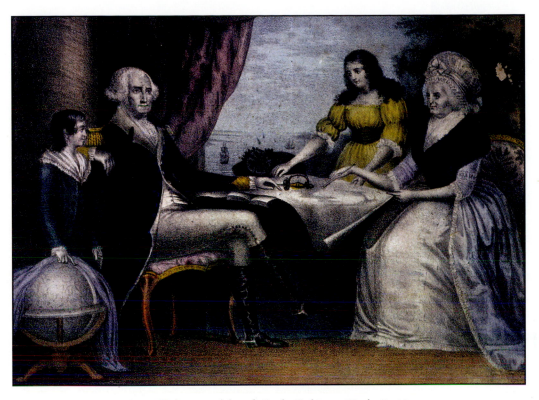

George Washington with his wife Martha Washington (Martha Custis),
often called Lady Washington, and family.

the Militia of the several States, when called into the actual Service of the United States; he may require the Opinion, in writing, of the principal Officer in each of the executive Departments, upon any Subject relating to the Duties of their respective Offices, and he shall have Power to grant Reprieves and Pardons for Offences against the United States, except in Cases of Impeachment.

"He shall have Power, by and with the Advice and Consent of the Senate, to make Treaties, provided two thirds of the Senate present concur; and he shall nominate, and by and with the Advice and Consent of the Senate, shall appoint Ambassadors, other public Ministers and Consuls, Judges of the supreme Court, and all other Officers of the United States, whose Appointments are not herein otherwise provided for, and which shall be established by Law: but the Congress may by Law vest the Appointments of such inferior Officers, as they think proper, in the President alone, in the Courts of Law, or in the Heads of Departments.

"The President shall have Power to fill up all Vacancies that may happen during the Recess of the Senate, by granting Commissions which shall expire at the End of their next Session.

"SECTION 3. He shall from time to time give to the Congress Information of the State of the Union, and recommend to their Consideration such Measures as he shall judge necessary and expedient; he may, on extraordinary Occasions, convene both Houses, or either of them, and in Case of Disagreement between them, with Respect to the Time of Adjournment, he may adjourn them to such Time as he shall think proper; he shall receive Ambassadors and other public Ministers; he shall take Care that the Laws be faithfully executed, and shall Commission all the Officers of the United States.

"SECTION 4. The President, Vice President and all civil Officers of the United States, shall be removed from Office on Impeachment for, and Conviction of, Treason, Bribery, or other high Crimes and Misdemeanors.

G. WASHINGTON—President and deputy from Virginia."

2

JOHN ADAMS (b.1735, d.1826)

Federalist. President 1797–1801

Vice president: Thomas Jefferson

An academically minded lawyer whose sure grasp of Constitutional issues both laid the groundwork for the United States' fledgling government, and secured his election as president, John Adams was born in 1735 in Braintree, Massachusetts, the descendant of British settlers. After studying for the ministry at Harvard, from which he graduated in 1755, he became a schoolmaster in Worcester and then studied law, being admitted to the bar in 1758.

Although a patriot whose ideals had been inflamed by the theories of his radical cousin, Sam Adams, and a leading agitator against the Stamp Act of 1765, Adams earned popular censure by successfully defending British soldiers who had been involved in the Boston Massacre.

During the War of Independence Adams became a leading figure at both the first and second Continental Congresses; it was he who seconded Lee's motion in favor of independence in 1776, and he also helped Jefferson edit the Declaration of Independence and then secure its adoption by the congress. Adams was the author of much of Massachusetts' state constitution of 1780 and of many papers that helped guide the Constitutional Convention. Adams furthermore served as a diplomat in France, Holland, and Britain between 1781 and 1788, in which capacity his crowning achievement was the successful negotiation of the 1783 Treaty of Paris, by which the United States' independence was formally recognized.

Adams had helped to obtain Washington's appointment as commander-in-chief of the revolutionary army, and between 1789 and 1797 he served as Washington's vice president. After Washington's decision not to seek a third term, Adams seemed the obvious choice as presidential successor, and he was elected over Thomas Jefferson in 1796. Although a moderate Federalist, like Washington, he tried to remain politically impartial, and stood aloof from Federalist and Republican wrangling, but thereby also alienated both factions.

Adam's presidency was dominated by France's lingering resentment that, despite its support of the colonies during the Revolution, the United States was now pursuing a policy of neutrality with regard to both Britain and France. France, too, had since undergone a revolution, and was now seizing any U.S. ships trading with Britain. Adam's initial overtures to the French resulted in his publication of Gallic demands that any cessation of harassment should be bought by the United States. As a result of French aggression Adams was responsible for the establishment of the Department of the Navy in 1798 to commission warships, and for thus creating the first credible U.S. Navy.

Faced with increasing French hostility, Adams incurred unpopularity when he passed the four Alien and Sedition Acts of 1798, which allowed him to banish or imprison foreigners, and which outlawed criticism of the government in an attempt to prevent the spread of subversive ideas from France. The acts were considered undemocratic, and enraged Jefferson's Republicans. Adams even reappointed the retired Washington as commander-in-chief of the U.S. armies in preparation for war, but effective opposition from the Federalist Alexander Hamilton caused Adams to abandon this policy in favor of sending diplomats to France instead. War was avoided by the signing of a treaty with France in 1800, which unfortunately also had the effect of infuriating the Federalists.

As a result of his inability to placate either political faction, Adams lost the 1800 presidential election to Vice President Jefferson. He retired to Braintree, where he resumed his academic studies and voluminous writing and correspondence. Adams lived long enough to see his son, John Quincy Adams, become president in 1825; he died on July 4, 1826—the 50th anniversary of the Declaration of Independence—a few hours after Jefferson.

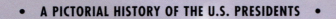

John Adams, the second president of the United States.

3.

THOMAS JEFFERSON (b.1743, d.1826)

Democratic-Republican. President 1801–1809

Vice presidents: Aaron Burr, George Clinton

The outstanding abilities of the multitalented Thomas Jefferson manifested themselves in the fields of law, philosophy, architecture, diplomacy, and writing—to name but a few—as well as politics. A passionate proponent of the natural rights of men, probably his most celebrated legacy is the Declaration of Independence—the world's most resounding statement of democratic freedom.

The son of a landowner, Jefferson was born in 1743 in Shadwell, Virginia. Before studying law he attended the College of William and Mary between 1760 and 1762; he was admitted to the bar in 1767. In common with Washington, Jefferson was a member of the Virginia House of Burgesses from 1769 to 1774. Influenced by Enlightenment ideas regarding natural rights, in 1774 he published *A Summary View of the Rights of British America*. Later, as a delegate at the Continental Congress, he is best remembered for drafting the Declaration of Independence of 1776, which asserted that all men are equal, that governments should serve the people, and that by failing to do so, they forfeit their authority.

After this momentous assertion of civic rights was adopted Jefferson retired to Virginia, where he served as state governor between 1779 and 1781. He was responsible for Virginia's Bill for Establishing Religious Freedom (enacted in 1786) and, despite being a slave-owner himself, campaigned for the abolition of the slave trade. In 1784 he was sent to France as a commissioner, later succeeding Franklin as minister plenipotentiary; during this five-year period Jefferson observed the awakening of revolutionary fever in France.

After his return to the U.S. in 1789, he became secretary of state in Washington's first administration, but a bitter feud with Alexander Hamilton over the latter's financial policies and his pro-British, anti-French stance, culminated in Jefferson's resignation in 1793. Two years later, however, Jefferson found himself vice president to John Adams (Jefferson had been defeated by Adams by a mere three votes), a position which he held until 1801. It was not a happy period, however, for the Republican Jefferson was opposed to Adams's Alien and Sedition Acts of 1798, which he regarded as being unconstitutional, and he additionally remained in conflict with Hamilton's Federalist faction.

Adams's unpopularity resulted in Jefferson's election as president in 1800; his vice president was Aaron Burr. His first term was a triumph, particularly in terms of foreign policy. A naval war against the Barbary pirates of Tripoli (1801–1805) resulted in the cessation of the U.S.A.'s payment of tribute, while in 1803 Jefferson presided over the purchase of the Louisiana Territory from France for $15 million, thereby doubling the size of the union. Politically, Jefferson provided firm leadership.

Reelected in 1804, with George Clinton as his vice president, Jefferson's second term of office was less successful. Burr was suspected of trying to seize an area of the Spanish Southwest for his own gain, and although Jefferson attempted to have him tried for treason Burr was acquitted. Britain, which was at war with Napoleonic France, was impressing U.S. sailors (seizing them as alleged deserters) and attacked the U.S. frigate, *Chesapeake*, in 1807. In an attempt to avoid war with Britain, in the same year Jefferson embargoed U.S. ships from exporting goods to both Britain and France, but this policy adversely affected U.S. trade and cost him much popularity, particularly in New England.

Jefferson retired in 1809 to "Monticello" in Virginia, the house which he had himself designed (the classically inspired campus of the University of Virginia that he founded in 1819 was also designed by him). Like his old friend and sometime adversary, John Adams, he died on Independence Day in 1826—a fitting date for such a zealous champion of human liberty.

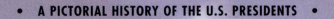

1743 _Th Jefferson_ 1826.
from the original portrait by Gilbert Stuart in possession
of Bowdoin College~Brunswick, Maine.

Thomas Jefferson, the principal author of the Declaration of Independence;
he became the third president of the United States.

4.

JAMES MADISON (b.1751, d.1836)

Democratic-Republican. President 1809–1817

Vice presidents: George Clinton, Elbridge Gerry

In common with his predecessors, James Madison, the fourth U.S. president, was a member of the "Virginia dynasty" that had presided over the birth of the new American nation. Among his many other achievements, Madison created the Library of Congress in 1783—now the world's largest collection of books. It is as the "Father of the Constitution," however, that he is mainly celebrated.

Born in 1751 in Port Conway, Virginia, the eldest son of an Orange County planter, Madison graduated from the College of New Jersey (now Princeton) in 1771, having absorbed many tenets of European Enlightenment thought. Although a nominal colonel of the militia during the Revolution, Madison never saw combat. He was elected a delegate to the Virginia legislature in 1776, where he helped to draft the Virginia constitution and also formed a lasting friendship with Thomas Jefferson; both men shared the same democratic ideals, and both were delegates at the two Continental congresses.

A member of Virginia's governor's council from 1777 to 1779, and subsequently a member of the House of Delegates, Madison continued to work with Governor Jefferson, helping to secure the passage of Jefferson's religious freedom bill. Imbued with a belief in a strong government, whose "separation of powers" would provide a series of checks and balances, Madison's views were instrumental in the drafting and adoption of the United States Constitution by the Constitutional Congress of 1787, earning him the venerable appellation "Father of the Constitution."

Madison was elected to the House of Representatives during Washington's first government, where he sponsored the Bill of Rights. Along with Jefferson, he opposed the Federalists, whose policies he deemed to be overly centralist and undemocratic. In 1797 the disenchanted Madison left Congress to devote much of his energy to opposing Adams's Alien and Sedition Acts, including drafting the Virginia Resolutions of 1798 in defense of civil liberty.

Serving as Jefferson's secretary of state from 1801, and also as a special envoy to France, during which time he negotiated the U.S. purchase of Louisiana, Madison was elected president in 1808. His status both as the "Father of the Constitution" and as a preeminent Republican leader made him a natural choice as Jefferson's successor.

Perhaps the greatest test that he faced was in the U.S.A.'s relationship with Britain. Since the time of Jefferson's second presidency British ships had been impressing into the British Navy U.S. sailors who could not prove their nationality. The Embargo Act of 1807 had failed to solve the problem, and popular anti-British feeling was rising to a crescendo. Despite Madison's attempts to settle the matter by means of diplomacy, the growing war fever could not be ignored, and in 1812 Madison somewhat reluctantly asked Congress to declare war on Britain—a move that resulted in his reelection in the same year. The war initially comprised a series of inconclusive naval skirmishes, and Madison was castigated for the corresponding loss of U.S. trade. The nadir came when British troops captured and burned Washington D.C. (including the Capitol and the White House) in 1814, but this humiliation was countered by the United States' resounding victory at Baltimore Harbor in 1814 (an event that inspired the writing of "The Star Spangled Banner").

The war was ended by the Treaty of Ghent in 1814, which concluded little, but a few weeks later, in 1815, the U.S.A. was basking in Andrew Jackson's victory at New Orleans, and Madison benefited from this national pride. The uneventful latter part of his presidency saw him charter the second National Bank, and also establish protective industrial tariffs.

Retiring from the presidency in 1816, Madison returned to Virginia to run his plantation and pursue his many other interests. He died in 1836.

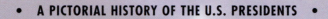

James Madison, fourth president of the United States. Madison is known as the "Father of the Constitution"
for his part in drafting the document at the Constitutional Convention of 1787 in Philadelphia, and in securing ratification for the document.

5.

JAMES MONROE (b.1758, d.1831)

Democratic-Republican. President 1817–1825

Vice president: Daniel D. Tompkins

The last of the "Virginia dynasty" of presidents, and a politician of rich and varied experience, James Monroe is best remembered for bequeathing his name to the doctrine that expressed the U.S.A.'s refusal to brook European interference in the Americas.

In common with Washington, Monroe was born in Westmoreland County, Virginia, in 1758, the son of a planter. Fired with revolutionary fervor, he abandoned his studies at the College of William and Mary for the Continental Army, in order to participate in the struggle for independence. He fought in many major battles, was wounded at Trenton in 1776, and was noted for his bravery.

In 1780 he returned to Virginia and studied law under Thomas Jefferson. Elected to the Virginia House of Delegates in 1782, he was also a member of the Confederation Congress between 1783 and 1786. Monroe became a senator in 1790, and during this period formed the Democratic-Republican Party with Jefferson and Madison. In 1794 he was appointed minister to France. Sympathizing with French revolutionary sentiments, his outspoken statements of support for them led to his recall to the U.S.A., after which he was elected governor of Virginia in 1799.

Recognizing his affinity with France, in 1803 Jefferson sent Monroe there to purchase the city of New Orleans, but instead Special Envoy Monroe, along with Minister Livingston, negotiated the purchase of Louisiana Territory for $15 million. This triumph was followed by a four-year period as minister to Britain. Monroe failed to beat Madison in the 1808 presidential election, after which he again became governor of Virginia in 1811, a position from which he resigned in 1812 in order to become secretary of state in Madison's administration. After the burning of Washington, D.C., in 1814, he was additionally appointed minister of war.

Monroe's vast political experience made him a natural choice as Madison's successor and in 1816 he was elected president. Benefiting from the general feeling of well-being that had prevailed during the latter years of Madison's presidency, Monroe faced few major tests. Initially, at least, he presided over a united Democratic-Republican Party, and managed to reconcile the previously troublesome Federalists. Unlike his predecessors, he was, moreover, spared the aggression of foreign powers, such as France and Britain. Such was his success that his first period in office was termed the "Era of Good Feelings."

Perhaps the most important issue of Monroe's first term was a diplomatic one. Andrew Jackson had pursued hostile Seminole Native Americans into Spanish Florida in 1818; having soothed Spanish outrage, Monroe was subsequently able to purchase Florida from Spain for $5 million. Just as he had been mainly responsible for the purchase of Louisiana Territory, Monroe had again significantly increased the size of the United States. Indeed, during his presidency, the number of U.S. states increased from 15 to 24. One controversial addition was Missouri, whose entry had been facilitated by Monroe's Missouri Compromise, for although Monroe was antislavery (Monrovia in Liberia is named after him), Missouri was a "slave state."

Monroe was reelected virtually unopposed in 1820. In 1823, in a damning response to a British initiative that Britain and the U.S.A. should discourage the involvement of other European nations in South America, he made a speech to Congress announcing his determination to prevent any European countries from creating new colonies in either North or South America. This famous declaration, which firmly asserted U.S. antipathy to any type of interference by the Old World in the New, became known as the Monroe Doctrine.

The impecunious Monroe retired in 1820 to Virginia, but moved to New York City in 1830. He died in the following year, on the same date as presidents Adams and Jefferson—July 4.

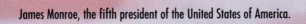

James Monroe, the fifth president of the United States of America.

6.

JOHN QUINCY ADAMS (b.1767, d.1848)

Democratic-Republican. President 1825–1829

Vice president: John C. Calhoun

A talented diplomat, linguist, and academic before his election to the office of president, and a diligent member of Congress afterward, Adams's term of office as the sixth president of the United States, which he termed "a harassing, wearying, teasing condition of existence," was the least happy period of his career.

The son of the U.S.A.'s second president, John Adams, John Quincy Adams was born in 1767 in Braintree, Massachusetts and was groomed for the premiership from birth. While accompanying his father to France, Holland, and Britain from the age of ten, Adams became fluent in French and Dutch; when still only a teenager he was appointed secretary to the mission to Russia between 1782 and 1783. He returned to the United States in 1785, graduating from Harvard in 1787, after which he studied law (he was admitted to the bar in 1790), and practiced in Boston. His early experience abroad made Adams ideally suited to a career as a diplomat, and between 1794 and 1797 he served as minister to Holland and later to Prussia (1797–1801).

Returning to Massachusetts in 1801 after his father's defeat by Jefferson in the presidential election of 1800, Adams practiced law until his election to the United States Senate in 1803. Initially a Federalist like his father, in 1807 he supported Jefferson's trade embargo, thus putting him firmly in the Democratic-Republican camp and forcing his subsequent resignation in 1808. He retreated to Harvard, where he was Boylston professor of oratory and rhetoric between 1806 and 1809, until Madison sent him to Russia as the U.S.A.'s first minister from 1809 to 1814. Adams chaired the peace negotiations that ended the war with Britain in 1814, and subsequently served as minister to Britain between 1815 and 1817.

As secretary of state in James Monroe's administration from 1817, Adams showed his brilliance in both negotiating the purchase of Florida and the Pacific Northwest from Spain in 1819, and in helping to draft the Monroe Doctrine in 1823. Perhaps one of the greatest incumbents of this position, he remained secretary of state until 1825.

Although he came second to Andrew Jackson in the presidential election of 1824, because there was no constitutional majority, Henry Clay's crucial vote resulted in Adams' election as president by the House of Representatives. When he then named Clay as secretary of state, the corresponding accusations of " corrupt bargain" caused a split in the Democratic-Republican Party. Adams was unfortunately unable successfully to apply his formidable negotiating skills to party politics, with disastrous consequences for his presidency.

Despite his enthusiastic plans for the creation of infrastructural improvements, such as a system of canals and highways, and for the consolidation and strengthening of government, Adams's presidency was dogged by party factionalism, by the continuing argument over national tariffs, and by the bitterly disputed question of slavery. By the time of the presidential election of 1828 Adams was so dispirited that he welcomed his comprehensive defeat by Andrew Jackson.

After his retirement to Braintree Adams was persuaded to reenter politics and was elected to the House of Representatives in 1830. Freed from the pressures of the presidency, Adams enjoyed his Congressional role, and lobbied in particular for the relaxation of slavery and for the retention of the Bank of the United States. A respected elder statesman, his debating skills led to him being nicknamed "Old Man Eloquent." His distinguished service to Congress continued until his death—in the House of Representatives itself—in 1848.

John Quincy Adams, the sixth president of the United States of America and the son of John Adams, the second president.

7.

ANDREW JACKSON (b.1767, d.1845)

Democrat. President 1829–1837

Vice presidents: John C. Calhoun, Martin Van Buren

The hero of the Battle of New Orleans, the charismatic Andrew Jackson broke the Virginia/Massachusetts presidential mold and brought a frontiersman's vigor to the office of president.

Jackson was born in 1767, in Waxhaw, South Carolina, to poor Northern Irish immigrants. Filled with a youthful spirit of adventure, in 1780 the now fatherless Jackson and his brother enlisted in the mounted militia of North Carolina. Captured by the British, for the rest of his life Jackson bore the scars that he incurred by refusing to clean a British officer's boots. Despite the privations of his early years Jackson later studied law, and was admitted to the bar in 1787, moving to Nashville, Tennessee, in 1788, where he enriched himself by speculating in land and slaves.

His political career began when he became a member of the Tennessee Constitutional Convention, and he was subsequently voted to the House of Representatives in 1796. He became a senator in 1797, but financial difficulties forced his return to Tennessee in 1798. Despite some distinctly unjudicial tendencies, such as fighting duels (in 1806 he killed Charles Dickinson, who had drawn attention to the fact that Rachel Robard's first marriage had not been annulled when she married Jackson), between 1798 and 1804 Jackson served as a justice of the supreme court of Tennessee.

Since 1802 major general of the Tennessee militia, Jackson was granted a similar rank in the U.S. volunteers on the outbreak of war with Britain in 1812. "Old Hickory's" first success was the defeat of the Creek Native Americans at the Battle of Horseshoe Bend in 1814, for which he was rewarded with a commission in the regular army. He was fêted as a national hero when he crushed the British at the Battle of New Orleans in 1815, but caused a crisis when he pursued a party of Seminole Native Americans into Spanish Florida in 1817. Happily for Jackson, the ultimate result of his incursion was the ceding of Florida to the United States in 1819.

In 1821 Jackson retired from soldiering and became governor of Florida; he resigned in the same year and was again elected to the Senate in 1823. Although he won the majority of votes in the presidential election of 1824, Jackson was ultimately defeated by John Quincy Adams, and retaliated by forming a formidable opposition to the president.

To popular rejoicing, Jackson won the 1828 election and promptly formed a controversial "kitchen cabinet" of allies. Claiming the necessity of "rotation in office," he actively implemented the "spoils system" by dismissing his opponents from federal jobs. Jackson's first term was further dominated by the rivalry between Van Buren and Vice President Calhoun. The "Nullification Crisis," caused when South Carolina threatened to secede from the Union if the duties that had been imposed by the tariff laws of 1828 and 1832 were collected, threatened to unseat Jackson; the president, however, reacted in ruthless fashion, sending troops and ships to Charleston. A compromise tariff in 1833 avoided further confrontation.

Jackson was reelected with a large majority in 1832. During his second term he continued his virulent opposition to the Bank of the United States, withdrawing government funds from it in 1833 (and thus precipitating a financial crisis). Although he recognized Texas's independence, Jackson refused to annex the state for fear of splitting the Democratic Party over slavery.

Ever popular with the people of the United States, who considered him one of them, Jackson retired to Tennessee in 1837, dying in 1845. His humble origins, moral courage, and his distrust of governmental authority and corrupt private interests have caused him to be regarded as a founding father of the modern Democratic Party.

Major general Andrew Jackson, later the seventh president of the United States of America,
with the Tennessee forces at Hickory Grounds, Alabama.

8

MARTIN VAN BUREN (b.1782, d.1862)

Democrat. President 1837–1841

Vice president: Richard M. Johnson

Although a consummate "machine" politician, Martin Van Buren served only one term as president, and that largely as a result of Andrew Jackson's endorsement.

The son of a farmer and tavern-keeper, and the descendent of Dutch immigrants, Van Buren was born in Kinderhook, New York, in 1782. Despite a lack of formal education, he had nevertheless learned enough to embark upon a successful law practice in 1803.

Van Buren's political career began when he served as surrogate between 1808 and 1813, which was followed by his election to the New York state senate in 1812. Power politics in Albany were then defined by the struggle between the followers of DeWitt Clinton and his opponents, the "Bucktails," of whom Van Buren became the leader. He was appointed attorney general in 1816, but was dismissed in 1819 when Clinton became governor. Undeterred, in 1821 Van Buren was elected to the United States Senate, to which he was reelected in 1827, and where he made his name as an opponent of John Quincy Adams.

During his early years in the political arena Van Buren, whose skills earned him the nicknames "Little Magician," and "Red Fox of Kinderhook," had become well versed in the machinations of politics, and his power base—termed the "Albany Regency"—which exploited the "spoils system" and united fellow Democrats Calhoun, Crawford, and Jackson, threw its considerable support behind the latter's bid for the presidency. Throughout his career Van Buren firmly believed that the two-party system, rather than fragmented factionalism, was the lifeblood of democracy.

Although he was successful in his bid for the governorship of New York in 1828, he resigned in 1829 when Jackson offered him the position of secretary of state. Despite their completely contrasting characters, the two built up a strong partnership, and when Jackson was reelected as president in 1832 Van Buren became his vice president in place of Calhoun, who had enraged Jackson by his trenchant stance on nullification.

On Jackson's retirement Van Buren, whom Jackson regarded as his natural successor, defeated the Whig William Henry Harrison in the presidential election of 1836. He was immediately faced with a testing crisis when Jackson's policy of disabling the Bank of the United States, along with expansion and the buying of land by speculators with paper money, culminated in economic depression and the "Panic" of 1837. Van Buren advocated creating an independent federal treasury that would give the government some financial independence; although this was established in 1840, it did little to help the business community or, indeed, the people.

The popularity that Van Buren had inherited from Jackson had been fatally eroded and in the presidential election of 1840 he lost heavily to Harrison. Like Jackson, Van Buren had refused to annex Texas, and after his defeat in 1842 he and the Whig Henry Clay agreed to continue to oppose this issue, on the pragmatic grounds of avoiding splitting both the Democratic and Whig factions. The result was the loss of Van Buren's nomination by the Democrats for the 1844 presidential election.

During his presidency Van Buren had taken a conciliatory stance over the perennially explosive issue of slavery, allowing its continuation in the South while predicting that: "The end of slavery will come." In the run-up to the presidential election of 1848 Van Buren's "Barnburners" supported the Wilmot Proviso, which advocated the nonextension of slavery. The subsequent rift with the Democratic Party again resulted in Van Buren's defeat by a Whig, Zachary Taylor.

Effectively retiring from politics after his latest defeat in the presidential election of 1848, Van Buren spent some years in Europe before returning to Kinderhook, where he died in 1862.

Martin Van Buren was the eighth president of the United States. He was known as the "Red Fox" or "Little Magician" for his canny politics, but condemned for his refusal to allow the government to interfere in the great depression or "Panic" of 1837. He formed the coalition that later became the modern Democratic Party.

9.

WILLIAM HENRY HARRISON (b.1773, d.1841)

Whig. President 1841-1841

Vice president: John Tyler

William Henry Harrison was a second-generation member of the "Virginia dynasty," a celebrated soldier, and the first Whig to become president. Sadly, as president he had no opportunity to prove his worth, for he was also the first to die in office—only a month after his inauguration.

Harrison, who was born in 1773 on Berkeley plantation, in Charles City County, Virginia, had an impeccable pedigree as far as candidacy for the presidency was concerned, for his father, Benjamin Harrison, had served in the Continental Congress and had been a signatory of the Declaration of Independence. Harrison initially considered his vocation to lie in medicine, and studied in Richmond and Philadelphia toward this end, but enlisted as an ensign in the First Regiment of Infantry in 1791. He eventually became a captain, and his early career included a commendation for bravery at the Battle of Fallen Timbers in 1794, as well as a period as the commandant of Fort Washington.

Harrison resigned from the army in 1798 and settled in North Bend, Ohio. President John Adams appointed him secretary of the Northwest Territory in the same year and in 1799 he was elected to Congress, where he supported the Land Act of 1800. His next position was as governor of Indiana Territory, a post that he held from 1801 to 1812. His governorship was marked by constant conflicts with Native Americans over the United States' settlement of Native American lands, and although Harrison attempted to placate them by peaceful means war almost inevitably ensued. His most famous encounter was with Shawnee chief Tecumseh and his brother, the Prophet, at the Battle of Tippecanoe in 1811; the battle was inconclusive, but nevertheless caught the public's imagination and catapulted "Old Tip" to national fame.

When the United States went to war against Britain Harrison was appointed brigadier general (later major general) of the Northwest forces in 1812. After withstanding the sieges of Fort Meigs and capturing Detroit, Harrison was instrumental in causing the defeat of the British and their Native American allies at the Battle of the Thames (in Ontario) of 1813, in which his old enemy, Tecumseh, was killed.

After resigning from the army in 1814, Harrison decided to capitalize on his military reputation and enter politics. He was a member of the United States House of Representatives from 1816 to 1819 and served on the Ohio state senate between 1819 and 1821. A U.S. senator for Ohio between 1825 and 1828, Harrison subsequently served as minister to Colombia, after which financial difficulties forced him to become clerk of the court of common pleas in Hamilton County, Ohio, in 1834.

Harrison, whose military fame was regarded by the Whigs as an effective counter to the Jacksonian Democrats, was defeated by Van Buren in the presidential election of 1836, but this result was overturned in the election of 1840. Perhaps the first genuine two-party election campaign, the run-up to the 1840 election was particularly notable for its campaign propaganda, in which the privileged Harrison was misleadingly, but energetically, portrayed as the "Log Cabin and Hard Cider" candidate. However absurd such propaganda, new election tactics like soundbites, touring, and an avoidance of real issues were so successful that they are now considered the prototype for all subsequent presidential campaigns.

Harrison had become president at the age of 68. Yet, exhausted by the relentless speechmaking and traveling that had formed such an important part of his campaign, he died of pneumonia after just 31 days in office. It was left to his grandson, Benjamin Harrison, to try to fulfill the family's expectations.

A painting by Albert Gallatin Hoit of William Henry Harrison.
Harrison was President of the United States in 1841 and died in office.

10.

JOHN TYLER (b.1790, d.1862)

Whig. President 1841–1845

Vice president: none

John Tyler was the first vice president to assume office after the death of the presidential incumbent; this unprecedented precipitation by tragedy to the United States' highest honor would subsequently recur on a number of occasions. His elevation also left the vice presidency vacant.

In common with William Henry Harrison, Tyler was born in Charles City County, Virginia, in 1790. His plantation-owning father, who was variously governor of Virginia from 1808 to 1811, speaker of the Virginia House of Delegates, and a judge, gave him a taste for politics, and Tyler was an early and eager participant. After graduating from William and Mary College at the age of 17, and being admitted to the bar at 19, he was elected to the Virginia House of Delegates at 21, as a Jeffersonian Democratic-Republican, and to the U.S. House of Representatives at 27. Appointed governor of Virginia in 1825, two years later he was elected to the United States Senate, where he remained until 1836.

A man of strong constructionist beliefs, and a fervent supporter of States' Rights—including its implicit acceptance of slavery—Tyler voted against the Missouri Compromise of 1820. Having been alienated by President Jackson's stance over the Nullification Crisis, his principles compelled him to resign from both the Senate and the Democratic Party in 1836, ostensibly to avoid having to vote in favor of expunging a censure of Jackson from the record.

His anti-Jacksonian stance endeared him to the Whigs, who additionally felt that his position on States' Rights would appeal to the South. In 1840 he was therefore nominated for the vice presidency and, along with Harrison, was strongly promoted in the "Log Cabin and Hard Cider," or "Tippecanoe and Tyler too" presidential campaign, which resulted in a Whig victory. A month after his inauguration, however, Harrison was dead, and after some discussion as to whether Tyler should be acting president or president in his own right he was sworn in at the age of 50—the youngest man to hold presidential office until then.

Although he is remembered for admitting Texas and Florida into the Union, Tyler's presidency was blighted by political conflict. So unpopular was his veto of Congress's Clay-inspired bills for the recreation of the Bank of the United States (which Tyler regarded as being unconstitutional) that in response his entire cabinet, apart from Daniel Webster, resigned in protest. Having thus enraged his party, from now on Tyler was doomed to having to fight a battle on every issue. Indeed, after he vetoed a bill for a protective tariff, Congress even resolved to impeach Tyler in 1842, but he evaded this by forcing Congress to pass separate, milder bills, and finally approved the tariff. The ongoing war was not won, however, and in 1845 Congress overrode a presidential veto for the first time.

Despite some successes, including sending a trade mission to China, reorganizing the navy, and instigating the "Log Cabin" bill, which allowed homesteaders to buy 160 acres of unsettled land, Tyler—nicknamed "His Accidency"—remained deeply unpopular. He was not nominated for reelection in 1844 and retired to Virginia.

In 1861 he chaired a peace commission that sought to find a solution to avoid the civil war that was brewing between North and South, but its failure led him to endorse secession, as a result of which Tyler was elected to the Confederate House of Representatives. In 1862, however, before he could take his seat, he died.

John Tyler, the tenth president of the United States, he assumed office following the death of William H. Harrison.

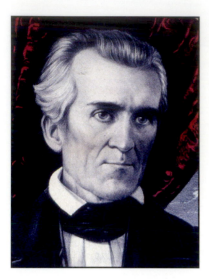

JAMES K. POLK (b.1795, d.1849)

Democratic. President 1845–1849

Vice president: George M. Dallas

After the ignominy of Tyler's term in office, the hard-working James Knox Polk, a man who believed in "manifest destiny," masterminded a spectacularly successful policy of territorial expansion for the United States, in the process restoring respect to the presidency.

Polk was born in 1795, near Pineville in North Carolina, to a pioneer family from Pennsylvania. His father, Samuel Polk, later speculated in land on the Tennessee frontier and moved his family to Columbia in 1806. Polk graduated from the University of North Carolina in 1818 and, after a period of studying law with Felix Grundy in Nashville, was admitted to the bar in 1820, whereupon he established his own legal practice in Tennessee.

Grundy had whetted Polk's appetite for politics, and in 1819 he helped the young man to obtain the clerkship of the state senate; in 1823 Polk was elected to the lower house. Voted to the United States House of Representatives for the first time in 1825, Polk served seven consecutive terms in Congress as a Democrat. As a family friend of Andrew Jackson Polk became a protégé of the president. Polk served as speaker of the House of Congress between 1835 and 1839 and demonstrated considerable skill in controlling Congress's frequently stormy debates. In a deliberate attempt to try to reconcile the state with Jackson, in 1839 Polk became governor of Tennessee, but failed to be reelected in both 1841 and 1843.

In his unexpected nomination as Democratic candidate for the presidency in 1844 Polk benefited from the disunity that characterized the party during the years of Tyler's presidency. Although the favorite, Van Buren was unable to secure enough votes during the party-convention ballots, and after the eighth indecisive ballot George Bancroft put forward Polk's name. Van Buren opposed the annexation of Texas, but Polk exploited his support of this popular action, with the result that Bancroft's "dark horse" was unanimously elected. During the subsequent presidential campaign, as well Texas's annexation Polk agitated for the U.S. occupation of Oregon Territory, which was then being disputed with Britain, and on this platform defeated the Whig candidate Henry Clay.

Following up his election promise, Polk entered into negotiations with Britain over Oregon and eventually compromised on a boundary of the 49th Parallel with British Canada (as opposed to the "Fifty-Four Forty [54° 41'] or Fight" that he had earlier advocated in an alliterative slogan). Other measures enacted during Polk's administration included the establishment of an independent treasury and the reduction of the tariff.

The major issue of Polk's presidency was, however, the Mexican War. The United States had finally decided to accede to Texas's demands to be annexed to the Union, but the outraged Mexico argued that Texas remained Mexican. Polk furthermore suggested that Mexico cede New Mexico and California to the United States. When Mexico refused, Polk sent General Zachary Taylor to the Rio Grande in 1846 with orders to provoke hostilities. Mexico resisted, and Polk obtained a declaration of war from Congress by claiming that Mexico had "shed American blood on American soil." By 1848 Mexico had been defeated and the resulting Treaty of Guadalupe Hidalgo augmented the United States with parts of Arizona, California (in which gold was discovered in 1848), Colorado, Nevada, New Mexico, Utah, and Wyoming—over half a million square miles—in exchange for $18,250,000. "Young Hickory" had triumphed, but the war had raised some thorny moral questions, for many felt that the U.S. should not have gained territory by means of aggressive tactics and armed force.

Despite his triumphs, the exhausted Polk decided not to seek reelection in 1848, and retired to Nashville, where he died in 1849.

James Knox Polk, the barrister and politician who became the 11th president of the United States in 1844.

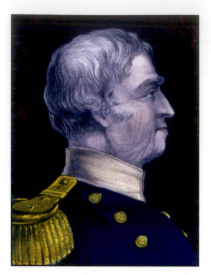

12.

ZACHARY TAYLOR (b.1784, d.1850)

Whig. President 1849–1850

Vice president: Millard Fillmore

Despite the fact that Zachary Taylor was the 12th president of the United States, he served for only a year, and "Old Rough and Ready" is instead more popularly remembered as the rugged hero of the Mexican War who never lost a battle.

Taylor was born near Barboursville, in Orange Country, Virginia, in 1784. His father had served as a lieutenant colonel during the War of Independence, and the young Taylor was inspired by stories of his father's exploits. He was commissioned a first lieutenant of infantry in 1808 and pursued a solidly military career for the next 40 years, rising gradually through the ranks and making a name for himself with his bravery and resourcefulness. During the war with Britain, in 1812 Captain Taylor defended Fort Harrison against Native American attacks and by 1815 had become a major. Having contributed to the successful conclusion of the Black Hawk War, in 1832, now a colonel, Taylor accepted the surrender of Chief Black Hawk himself. He also participated in the Seminole Wars, seeing action at the Battle of Okeechobee in 1837 and being breveted brigadier general in 1838, with the command of all U.S. troops in Florida.

Up to 1846 Taylor had undoubtedly been regarded as a gifted soldier, but it was the Mexican War that really made his reputation. Sent by President Polk with 4,000 men to the Rio Grande—the disputed border between Texas and Mexico—with orders to provoke the Mexicans into an aggressive reaction. Taylor accomplished this aim by blockading the town of Matamoras from the newly constructed Fort Texas. Mounting a spirited defense against the furious Mexican response, Taylor had already won the battles of Palo Alto and Resaca de la Palma before Congress officially declared war, and he also laid siege to Monterrey. Because Monterrey was not an out-and-out victory, however, Polk began to favor General Winfield Scott, but Major General Taylor soon restored the presidential confidence. In 1847 he was attacked at Buena Vista by a Mexican force four times greater than his own, under the command of General Santa Anna. Resisting fiercely, Taylor finally forced a Mexican retreat, to widespread U.S. jubilation.

After Polk's decision not to stand for reelection in 1848 the Whigs saw Taylor as a popular choice with which to replace him—after all, the militaryhero ticket had worked for both Jackson and Harrison. Thus the man who had never once voted was duly swept to victory in the first election to be held simultaneously in every state.

The new president found himself faced with the knotty problem of whether the new states of California and New Mexico should be admitted to the Union as free or slave states. Although he was himself a slave-owner, and despite the fact that he believed that slavery should be retained in existing slave states, Taylor did not advocate the adoption of slavery in the new territories. The "President's Plan" caused profound Southern dissension, but Taylor made it clear that he would hold the Union together by every means necessary.

Less controversially, Taylor signed the Clayton-Bulwer Treaty with Britain, which provided for joint control of a proposed canal in Nicaragua. He had little time to do more, however, for in 1850—just a year after his inauguration—and with the slavery issue still unresolved he died of cholera.

Zachary Taylor, American general and the 12th president of the U.S.A.

13.

MILLARD FILLMORE (b.1800, d.1874)

Whig. President 1850–1853

Vice president: none

Like John Tyler before him, Millard Fillmore found himself unexpectedly elevated to the presidency in 1850. Unfortunately for Fillmore, he had inherited the apparently insurmountable problem of slavery that had dominated Zachary Taylor's short administration, and lacked the authority to deal with it either effectively or decisively.

Fillmore was born into poverty in Locke, Cayuga County, New York, in 1800. The Fillmore family was not wealthy enough to educate the boy and he was apprenticed to a carder and cloth-dresser at the age of 14, later buying himself out for $30. Fillmore, however, was determined to get an education, and in 1819 enrolled in an academy in New Hope, in the same year becoming a clerk in a judge's office and beginning to study law. Over the following years he taught school and clerked in a law firm until, in 1823, he was admitted to the bar and subsequently set up his own legal practice.

Although he had previously displayed little interest in politics, in 1828 Fillmore was elected to the New York state assembly as an anti-Masonic representative; during his three terms in Albany he attracted the greatest notice for engineering the abolition of the imprisonment of debtors. He was subsequently elected an anti-Masonic member of Congress in 1832 and became a Whig Congressman in 1836, in which capacity he served three terms. As chairman of the Ways and Means Committee between 1840 and 1842 he was responsible for securing the adoption by Congress of the tariff of 1842.

Persuaded to run for the governorship of New York in 1844, rather than as Henry Clay's running mate in the presidential election the same year, Fillmore lost to Silas Wright. He served as New York's comptroller-general from 1847, but in 1848 was nominated as vice president by the Whig Party, which pragmatically regarded him as an attractive counterbalance to Zachary Taylor.

In 1848 Fillmore duly became vice president and, on Taylor's sudden death in 1850, president. The debate over the status of New Mexico and California had not been conclusively resolved by Taylor, and Fillmore himself favored the Compromise of 1850. This set of laws allowed California to enter the Union as a free state and restricted the slave trade in the District of Columbia. Territorial governments were furthermore created in Utah and New Mexico, in order to allow these states to decide the slavery issue for themselves. The harsh Fugitive Slave Act, which was also approved by Fillmore, enraged antislavery campaigners by its demand for the forced return of runaway slaves. In his affirmation of States' Rights and his attempt to appease all factions Fillmore had managed temporarily to shelve the crisis over slavery, but abolitionist sentiments had by no means been appeased.

On a happier note, Fillmore was responsible for authorizing Commodore Matthew Perry's mission to Japan between 1852 and 1854—so successful was Perry that the previously isolated Japan signed a treaty with the United States in 1854, thereby opening two ports to U.S. trading ships.

As a result of profound Northern dissatisfaction over Fillmore's handling of the slavery question, in 1852 Fillmore lost the Whig presidential nomination to Winfield Scott. He stood for reelection in 1856 for the nativist Know-Nothing Party, but came in a hopeless third to James Buchanan and John Frémont. Thereafter he devoted himself to a life of civic activity, which included founding the Buffalo General Hospital. He died in Buffalo, New York, in 1874.

Millard Fillmore, who became 13th president of the United States in 1850 when Zachary Taylor died of cholera.

14.

FRANKLIN PIERCE (b.1804, d.1869)

Democrat. President 1853–1857

Vice president: William R. D. King

Continuing Fillmore's policy of compromise and appeasement, Franklin Pierce tried to tread a middle line over slavery, but was accused of harboring Southern sympathies and proslavery partiality. Derided as being weak and shallow, Pierce was certainly not up to the challenges of this difficult period.

Unlike his predecessor, Pierce, who was born in 1804 in Hillsboro Lower Village, New Hampshire, came from a privileged background: his father, Benjamin Pierce, who had served as a general in the Revolutionary Army, was also governor of New Hampshire. Pierce graduated from Bowdoin College in 1824, was admitted to the bar in 1827, and then established a prosperous legal practice in Concord. In 1829, the same year in which his father began his second term of governorship, the younger Pierce was elected to the New Hampshire general court, where he acted as speaker in 1831 and 1832, before being voted to Congress as a Democratic representative in 1833.

In 1837, at the age of 33, Pierce became the youngest member of the United States Senate, but resigned in 1842 on the urging of his wife, Jane Means Appleton, who abhorred both politics and the hard-drinking lifestyle that went with it. Back in Concord, Pierce managed New Hampshire's Democratic campaigns so smoothly that President Polk appointed him federal district attorney in 1846. Refusing offers of political office in favor of seeing action in the Mexican War, Pierce, who enlisted as a private, was eventually commissioned a brigadier general. Although wounded in the Battle of Churubusco in 1847, he continued to command his troops until the capture of Mexico City.

Another "dark-horse" candidate, Pierce was nominated for the presidency in 1852, but only after the Democratic convention had held 49 ballots. Perceived as a compromise candidate who, although Northern, had Southern sympathies, and who furthermore was adept at charming voters, "Young Hickory of the Granite Hills" soundly defeated his former commander, General Winfield Scott, in the presidential election. Triumph was tempered with tragedy, however, for in early 1853 Pierce's only surviving child was killed in a train accident; it has been suggested that his grief hampered the new president's competency.

During his presidency, the U.S.A. experienced an economic boom, boosted by the treaty with Japan of 1854 which resulted from Commodore Perry's mission. In addition, Pierce enlarged the territory of the United States by means of the Gadsden Purchase, by which 29,000 square miles of land were acquired from Mexico.

Fillmore had attempted to resolve the bitter debate over slavery by means of the Compromise of 1850, but his conciliatory policy had settled nothing. Pierce created a storm of outrage when he partially revoked the Missouri Compromise of 1820 (which had allowed Missouri to enter the Union as a slave state) by signing the Kansas-Nebraska Act of 1854, which in creating these new states allowed them to decide for themselves whether they should be "slave" or "free." When civil war broke out in Kansas between the rival slavery and Free Soil factions Pierce was furthermore accused of supporting the Lecompton, proslave government. Further controversy raged when the leaked contents of the Ostend Manifesto of 1854 revealed Pierce's intention either to buy Cuba from Spain or to annex it should a slave revolt in Cuba spread to the American South.

Pierce was not nominated for reelection in 1856 and retired from politics in 1857. Apart from his attack on Lincoln, in which Pierce charged the president with fostering the Civil War, he lived out the rest of his life in relative obscurity, dying in 1869.

The 14th president of the United States, Franklin Pierce.

15.

JAMES BUCHANAN (b.1791, d.1868)

Democrat. President 1857–1861

Vice president: John C. Breckenridge

Although a capable diplomat, James Buchanan was unable to bring his skills of mediation to bear on the bitter North/South divide..By the end of his presidency Civil War was inevitable, and Buchanan was made the scapegoat on its outbreak.

Born in Cove Gap, near Mercersburg, Pennsylvania, in 1791, Buchanan graduated from Dickinson College in 1809 and was admitted to the bar in 1813, after which he set up his own law practice in Lancaster, Pennsylvania. Having served in the war against Britain in 1812, Buchanan entered politics as a Federalist in 1814 when he was elected to the Pennsylvania assembly, remaining there for two years. After being voted to the House of Representatives in 1821, Buchanan served for five terms until 1831; between 1832 and 1834 he acted as minister to Russia and negotiated a groundbreaking trade treaty in this position. On his return to the United States he was elected to the Senate and served as a senator until 1845.

Appointed secretary of state by President Polk during the Mexican War, Buchanan subsequently retired to Lancaster in 1848, intending to run for president in the 1852 presidential election. After he failed to be nominated he was sent to Britain as United States' minister by President Pierce, serving in this capacity from 1853 to 1856. As the author of the Ostend Manifesto of 1854 Buchanan was considered by the Southern states to be sympathetic to their cause, although, in fact, he was personally opposed to slavery. Along with his moderate politics, his absence from the United States during the time of the enactment of the Kansas–Nebraska Act of 1854 and its aftermath were perceived by the Democrats as desirable conciliatory advantages at a time of virulent extremism, and he was nominated for the presidency. On winning the presidential election of 1856 by a large majority in the Electoral College, Buchanan found the Southern states solidly behind him.

The North was outraged when the Supreme Court's explosive Dred Scott Decision proclaimed that slaves and their descendants were chattels, not citizens, and that Congress would be acting illegally if it deprived white citizens of their "property." In 1859 the abolitionist John Brown, raided an arsenal at Harper's Ferry, Virginia, hoping thus to arm slaves. He was captured and hanged, whereupon he simultaneously became both a symbol of abolition and a menacing specter of potential slave rebellion.

The dispute over Kansas that had marred Pierce's presidency continued into Buchanan's term of office. Like Pierce, Buchanan was accused of favoring the South, but, more pertinently in this context, he was determined strictly to abide by the law. Eventually Buchanan signed the English bill, which admitted Kansas into the Union in 1861 as a slave state, but with a reduced federal land grant. Congress became increasingly uncooperative, and by 1861 the unpopular Buchanan was in an impossible situation, and decided not to seek reelection.

At the first 1860 Democratic convention proslavery Southern delegates walked out to form their own convention, leading to the nomination for the presidency of two opposing Democratic candidates: John C. Breckenridge and Stephen A. Douglas. As a result, the Republican Abraham Lincoln was elected president in 1860, precipitating the secession of South Carolina from the Union in that year and that of seven Deep South states early in 1861. At the end of Buchanan's presidency, however, eight slave states remained within the Union, and although Civil War did not erupt until Lincoln's presidency it was Buchanan upon whom most of the blame for its outbreak was heaped. During his retirement in Pennsylvania Buchanan remained a supporter of the Union. He died in 1868.

James Buchanan, the Democratic candidate who became the 15th president of the United States.
It was during his administration that events escalated toward the American Civil War.

16.

ABRAHAM LINCOLN (b.1809, d.1865)

Republican. President 1861–1865

Vice presidents: Hannibal Hamlin, Andrew Johnson

Abraham Lincoln's presidency was marked by unprecedented violence: during his two terms of office the Civil War began and ended, and only five days after its conclusion Lincoln himself was assassinated. Although sometimes vilified by his contemporaries, today Lincoln is regarded as perhaps the United States' greatest president, who, with his honesty, integrity, and humanity, provided outstanding moral leadership.

Born near Hodgenville, Kentucky, in 1809, when Lincoln was seven his impoverished family moved to the Indiana frontier. The young Lincoln worked the land to help to support his family, and despite having had only a year of schooling demonstrated an insatiable desire for learning. He moved to New Salem, Illinois, in 1831, and in 1832 enlisted in the militia to fight in the Black Hawk War, but saw no action.

Lincoln was elected to the Illinois legislature in 1834. At the same time he taught himself law and was licensed in 1836. He practiced law after he left the Illinois state assembly in 1842, in the process earning himself the nickname "Honest Abe." In 1846 Lincoln was elected to the United States House of Representatives as a Whig, but returned, disillusioned, to Springfield, Illinois, in 1849. His vehement opposition to the Kansas-Nebraska Act of 1854, however, reawakened his interest in politics, and his antislavery convictions led him to join the newly formed Republican Party in 1856. In 1858 he challenged Stephen A. Douglas for the Senate and the pair debated slavery fiercely throughout Illinois. Despite his eloquence, Lincoln lost to Douglas.

Nominated Republican candidate for the presidency in 1860, Lincoln benefited from the division of the Democratic Party and was voted the first Republican president in the same year. His election, however, prompted the secession of several Southern states and by the time of Lincoln's inauguration only eight remained within the Union. Despite his statement that he would not abolish slavery and wished to hold the Union together, when a Confederate general, Beaureguard, opened fire on Fort Sumter in Charleston in April 1861 Lincoln swiftly called for militia volunteers to suppress the Confederate rebellion, suspended *habeas corpus* for secessionists, and blockaded the South by sea. In response, four more Southern states seceded; the United States was divided and at war with itself.

A speedy conclusion to the Civil War was expected, but the First Battle of Bull Run in July 1861 exposed the military weakness of the North: Southern commanders, such as Lee, Jackson, and Bragg consistently demonstrated their superiority over their Northern counterparts Scott, McClellan, Hooker, and Pope. Further Union defeats included the bloody Battle of Antietam in 1862.

In 1863 Lincoln presented the Emancipation Proclamation, by which all slaves in the Confederate states were pronounced free; the war was now being fought over moral and ideological issues, not merely over political secession. Later that year the Union Army won a resounding victory at Gettysburg (Lincoln's Gettysburg Address remains a world-famous pronouncement of democratic purpose, see page 47) and with the success of General Ulysses S. Grant in 1864, the tide seemed to have turned in the Union's favor.

The presidential election of 1864 saw Lincoln's reelection in doubt. Military successes in Atlanta and at Mobile Bay were, however, translated into political victory and Lincoln was again inaugurated, on March 4, 1865, urging "kindness toward all, with malice toward none." The surrender of the Confederate General Robert E. Lee on April 9, 1865, at Appomattox brought the Civil War to an end, and Lincoln prepared to reconstruct the nation. On April 14, however, he was shot by John Wilkes Booth at a theater and died the next day. He was mourned by most of the North, and also by many of his Southern opponents.

Abraham Lincoln, the 16th president of the United States, photographed only three days before his assassination.

IN THIS TEMPLE
AS IN THE HEARTS OF THE PEOPLE
FOR WHOM HE SAVED THE UNION
THE MEMORY OF ABRAHAM LINCOLN
IS ENSHRINED FOREVER

A marble statue of Abraham Lincoln at the Lincoln Memorial in Washington D.C.

A painting depicting Abraham Lincoln at work cutting logs. This early work gained him the nickname of "Railsplitter" when he entered politics.

The Gettysburg Address

"Four score and seven years ago our fathers brought forth, upon this continent, a new nation, conceived in Liberty, and dedicated to the proposition that all men are created equal.

"Now we are engaged in a great civil war, testing whether that nation, or any nation, so conceived, and so dedicated, can long endure. We are met here on a great battlefield of that war. We have come to dedicate a portion of it as a final resting place for those who here gave their lives that that nation might live. It is altogether fitting and proper that we should do this.

"But in a larger sense we can not dedicate—we can not consecrate—we can not hallow—this ground. The brave men, living and dead, who struggled here, have consecrated it, far above our poor power to add or detract. The world will little note, nor long remember, what we say here, but can never forget what they did here. It is for us, the living, rather to be dedicated here to the unfinished work which they have, thus far, so nobly carried on. It is rather for us to be here dedicated to the great task remaining before us—that from these honored dead we take increased devotion to that cause for which they gave the last full measure of devotion—that we here highly resolve that these dead shall not have died in vain, that this nation shall have a new birth of freedom; and that this government of the people, by the people, and for the people, shall not perish from the earth."

Abraham Lincoln, November 19, 1863.

17.

ANDREW JOHNSON (b.1808, d.1875)

Union-Democrat. President 1865–1869

Vice president: none

It was Andrew Johnson's misfortune that on the assassination of Lincoln it fell to him to confront the aftermath of the Civil War. Lacking Lincoln's stature and broad-mindedness, Johnson's unpopular measures led to his impeachment, as well as to the dramatic erosion of presidential power.

Johnson was born in Raleigh, North Carolina, in 1808. His father died when he was three and his mother struggled to bring up her two sons alone. Apprenticed to a tailor at the age of 14, Johnson did not receive the luxury of schooling but was nevertheless determined to educate himself. In 1827 he moved to Greeneville, Tennessee, where he opened a tailor's shop. He became active in local politics, rising from being a member of the town council in 1829 to mayor in 1830. His espousal of Democratic principles led to his election to the state legislature in 1835, 1839, and 1841, and then to Congress in 1843. He was gerrymandered out of Congress in 1852, however, but twice won the governorship of Tennessee (in 1853 and 1857), before being elected to the U.S. Senate in 1857. As a senator Johnson found himself torn between his support for States' Rights and his personal ambivalence to slavery; when he tried to prevent Tennessee's secession in 1860 he alienated the Democrats, as well as much of Tennessee.

Despite the fact that he represented a Southern state, on the outbreak of the Civil War in 1861 Johnson announced his intention to support the Union—the only Southern senator to do so. He was applauded by the North, but his family was forced to flee Tennessee. As a reward for his courageous stance Lincoln appointed Johnson military governor of Tennessee in 1862, where he worked hard to try to restore civil government. He was chosen as Lincoln's running mate in the 1864 presidential election precisely because he was a Southern Democrat: the conciliatory and successful Lincoln-Johnson ticket was designed to represent both North and South.

Sworn in as president on the day of Lincoln's death, April 15, 1865, Johnson proved himself unequal to the delicate task of reconstructing the Union. As well as possessing a fundamentally Southern mindset, as a constructionist his moderate instructions regarding the requirements for the readmission of the Southern states into the Union alienated Northern congressmen, who believed that Johnson had failed to protect African-American civil rights. They accordingly refused to seat any Southern representatives.

Johnson was convinced that Congress was acting unconstitutionally, and in 1866 vetoed three Congressional bills designed to protect the rights of former slaves; he also refused to endorse an amendment to the Constitution that gave African-Americans the right of citizenship. In response Congress overrode the presidential vetoes and furthermore enacted the Tenure of Office bill, which removed the president's power to dismiss officials appointed by Congress. In 1867 Congress set aside the Southern governments in favor of military governors, causing the furious Johnson actively to encourage Southern resistance.

Johnson's nadir came in 1868, when he dismissed Edwin M. Stanton, the secretary of state for war, for insisting that Southern military governors were answerable only to Congress. In consequence the Radical Republicans, led by Thaddeus Stevens, succeeded in impeaching the president for breach of the Tenure of Office Act. Johnson survived by a single vote, but left office in 1869 an embittered man. During his administration he had presided over only two successes: the purchase of Alaska from Russia in 1867 and the removal of French forces from Mexico in 1866.

Johnson retired to Tennessee, but reentered politics on his election to the Senate in 1874. He died shortly afterward, in 1875.

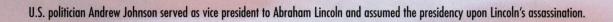

U.S. politician Andrew Johnson served as vice president to Abraham Lincoln and assumed the presidency upon Lincoln's assassination.

18.

ULYSSES S. GRANT (b.1822, d.1885)

Republican. President 1869–1877

Vice presidents: Schuyler Colfax, Henry Wilson

Ulysses S. Grant is remembered more for his brilliant leadership and masterly strategy during the Civil War than for his presidency, and, indeed, "Unconditional Surrender Grant" was more successful as a general than as the United States' 18th president.

Born Hiram Ulysses Grant in 1822, in Point Pleasant, Ohio, Grant was no great scholar and was uninterested in his family's tanning business. His father therefore obtained his entry to West Point in 1839 (into which he was mistakenly enrolled as Ulysses Simpson Grant—an appellation that he subsequently retained), where he spent four unhappy years excelling in little but horsemanship.

After West Point Grant was commissioned brevet second lieutenant in the 4th U.S. Infantry. Despite his abhorrence for the principles for which he believed the United States was fighting the Mexican War (1846–1848), Grant took part in many major battles and demonstrated an aptitude for command. Posted to Fort Vancouver on the West Coast in 1852, Captain Grant found separation from his family too much to bear and resorted to drink; he resigned from the army in 1854. Life as a civilian did not suit Grant either, however, and after his farming and real-estate ventures failed, he moved to Galena, Illinois, in 1860 to work as a clerk for his father.

His life seemed to have lost direction, but the outbreak of the Civil War gave Grant new purpose. He volunteered for the Union Army and in 1861 was appointed brigadier general of the volunteers by President Lincoln. His early successes included the capture of Fort Donelson and Fort Henry in 1862, after which he was created major general of volunteers. Despite routing the Confederates, Grant incurred vehement censure over his actions at Shiloh in

1862; Lincoln defended him, proclaiming "I can't spare this man—he fights," but Grant was sidelined until the Siege of Vicksburg in 1863 rehabilitated his reputation. Victory at Chattanooga in 1863 resulted in his appointment to the rank of lieutenant general, and in 1864 Grant assumed command of the Union Army. The latter part of his military career comprised a punishing campaign against Robert E. Lee and the army of Northern Virginia, and after Lee surrendered at Appomatox on April 9, 1865, Grant was lauded for his magnanimity.

Promoted to full general after the Civil War, in 1867 Grant served as secretary of war following Johnson's dismissal of Stanton, but resigned after five months. Grant himself was a popular Republican choice for president and was duly elected in 1868. The gritty military commander, was, however, a naïve and passive politician. He incurred criticism for promoting his personal friends and political benefactors to office and his first administration was tarnished by scandal, such as that of the Crédit Mobilier in 1872. Grant was reelected in 1872—largely thanks to the continuing adulation of the populace—but again his presidency was tainted by the corruption of those around him: his private secretary was exposed as being involved in the "Whiskey Ring," while his secretary of war attempted to defraud the Indian Agency. Grant did not strengthen his position by his loyal, but shortsighted, support of the transgressors.

Although he unsuccessfully sought a third, unprecedented, term in 1876, and again in 1880, Grant effectively retired in 1877 and embarked on a world tour. After his return to New York he faced financial ruin and was reduced to selling his swords as war souvenirs, but also wrote his celebrated *Personal Memoirs*. Although Congress restored his rank and voted him a salary, he died shortly afterward, in 1885.

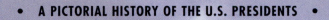

Ulysses Simpson Grant, a Civil War soldier and later the 18th President of the United States.

Ulysses S. Grant pictured in military uniform with his wife.

Right: The tomb of Ulysses S. Grant on Riverside Drive in Manhattan, New York City.

21.

CHESTER A. ARTHUR (b.1829, d.1886)

Republican. President 1881–1885

Vice president: none

Despite the fact that he himself had been removed from an influential position of patronage by President Hayes in 1878, as president Chester A. Arthur was responsible for reforming the "spoils system" that pervaded the civil service, and his honest administration caused Mark Twain to comment that "it would be hard to better."

Officially born in North Fairfield, Vermont, in 1829, it is possible that Arthur actually came into the world in Canada (which would have made him ineligible for the presidency). His father was an Irish immigrant who had worked as a teacher before becoming a Baptist minister. Arthur attended Union College in Schenectady, New York. After graduation in 1848 he taught school and became principal of the Cohoes Academy. Simultaneously studying law, he was later admitted to the bar in 1854 and established his own legal firm in New York City in 1856.

Arthur soon became involved in the local politics of New York City and supported the young Republican Party. As a result of his support for Governor Edwin D. Morgan, in 1860 Arthur was appointed New York's engineer-in-chief. Following the outbreak of the Civil War, in 1861 Arthur became assistant quartermaster general of the New York militia and was promoted to quartermaster general in 1862. From 1863 Arthur worked closely with Senator Roscoe Conkling, the head of New York's Republican Party machine and, in 1871, as a reward for his services to Conkling, was appointed port collector of New York City's Customs House. Although some claimed that he merely turned a blind eye, Arthur took full advantage of his position to promote his friends, which resulted in his suspension by Hayes in 1878. Undaunted by this setback, Arthur continued to run the Republican Party in New York City, in conjunction with Conkling.

Arthur was the "Stalwart" choice for nomination as Ulysses S. Grant's vice president at the 1880 Republican convention, when, despite Conkling's objections, party divisions resulted in Grant's replacement by James Garfield. The Garfield-Arthur team triumphed at the 1880 presidential election, and as vice president Arthur acceded to Conkling's demands that he be consulted on federal appointments in New York State. Garfield, however, did not concur, and Conkling resigned his Senate seat in protest. After Garfield's death at the hands of a "Stalwart" fanatic Arthur was inaugurated on September 20, 1881, to the obvious delight of his New York Republican cronies.

Given his previous record regarding the patronage system, as well as his close connection with the undoubtedly corrupt Conkling, it was widely expected that Arthur would abandon Hayes and Garfield's attempts to reform the civil service. Indeed, he conferred appointments on many "Stalwarts," causing one commentator to observe that Arthur's strategy was to "gobble all the vacancies for his particular friends and to talk reform at every gobble." Arthur, however, was determined to put an end to the issue that had marred the presidencies of his two predecessors. Declaring that appointments "should be based upon a certain fitness," he rose above partisanship to meet the challenge. The Pendelton Civil Service Act of 1883 created the politically neutral Civil Service Commission, classified all federal positions, and introduced a system of competitive examinations to ensure that all officeholders were qualified for their jobs.

Not surprisingly, Arthur's reforming stance, particularly over the prosecution of the Star Route fraudsters, earned the enduring antipathy of many of his fellow Republicans in Congress and he was not renominated in 1884. Arthur suffered from Bright's disease (a kidney complaint), and the sick man retired to New York, where he practiced law until his death in 1886.

A portrait of Chester A. Arthur, the 21st U.S. president.

22. & 24.

GROVER CLEVELAND (b.1837, d.1908)

Democrat. President 1885–1889, 1893–1897

Vice presidents: Thomas A. Hendricks, Adlai E. Stevenson

The only president to serve two nonconsecutive terms, to Grover Cleveland is accorded the distinction of being both the 22nd and 24th president of the United States. He is furthermore remembered as a reformer and as a man of integrity.

Cleveland was a man of moral rectitude, whose only known transgression was the fathering of an illegitimate child. The son of a Presbyterian minister, Cleveland was born in 1837, in Caldwell, New Jersey. After his father's death in 1853 Cleveland's uncle secured him a clerking position in a Buffalo law firm. He set up his own practice in 1859 and developed an interest in politics, working as a Democratic wardworker, assistant district attorney, and then as sheriff of Erie County. He was elected mayor of Buffalo in 1881 on an anticorruption platform and governor of New York in 1882, in which position the "veto governor" earned a reputation as an honest opponent of corruption and as a supporter of free enterprise.

His popularity with both Republican and Democratic businessmen resulted in Cleveland's nomination as Democratic candidate for the presidency, and the sharp divisions in the Republican Party (which led to the defection of the "Mugwumps") helped him to a narrow, but long-awaited, Democratic victory over James G. Blaine in 1884. Although he extended the civil-service merit system by repealing the Tenure of Office Act in 1887, during his first term of office party pressure compelled Cleveland to replace many Republican civil servants with Democrats, while he furthermore resisted Republican demands to provide information on political dismissals. Cleveland also vetoed excessive pension demands for Civil War veterans, in an effort both to control public spending, and to curb fraudulent claims.

His free-enterprise convictions led Cleveland to try to reduce the high tariff in 1887; the subsequent Mills Act of 1888 was too moderate, however, to be effective.

Although Cleveland won the popular vote, he lost the 1888 presidential election to the protectionist Republican Benjamin Harrison and returned to New York City to practice law. In 1892, however, Cleveland was reelected, and thus became the only president to serve two separate terms.

Cleveland's second administration coincided with a period of national economic difficulty. By the time of the Panic of 1893 the United States was in the grip of deep economic depression; four million Americans were unemployed and the increasing popular unrest was manifesting itself by means of such protests as the march of Coxey's Army in 1894. Cleveland tried to ameliorate the situation by attempting to reform the trade tariff, but was frustrated by Congressional opposition. The repeal of the Sherman Silver Purchase Act put the United States on the gold standard, but as a result Cleveland was forced to exchange government bonds for enormous stocks of gold from the industrialist J. P. Morgan. Further damage to his popularity was caused when he sent federal soldiers to Chicago to restore mail and railroad operations during the American Railway Union's Pullman Strike of 1894. The sole undisputed success of Cleveland's second administration was his reconciliation of Britain to U.S. arbitration over the disputed boundary between British Guiana and Venezuela in 1895.

By the time of the presidential election of 1896 Cleveland had become universally unpopular and lost the Democratic nomination to William J. Bryan, who accused him of "crucify[ing] mankind upon a cross of gold." He retired to Princeton, New Jersey, where he lectured and wrote until his death in 1908.

Grover Cleveland, the 22nd and 24th president of the United States of America. He was the first Democratic president to be elected after the Civil War but within a year of his taking office for the second time, four million people were unemployed and the country was bankrupt.

23.

BENJAMIN HARRISON (b.1833, d.1901)

Republican. President 1889–1893

Vice president: Levi P. Morton

In his election to the White House Benjamin Harrison followed in the footsteps of his grandfather, William Henry Harrison, the ninth president of the United States, who served in this capacity for only a month. In common with his forebear, Harrison had seen military service; unlike his Whig grandfather, however, his politics were Republican.

Despite William Henry Harrison's distinguished army record, his grandson, who was born in North Bend, Ohio, in 1833, eschewed a military career in favor of the law. He attended Cary Academy (later Farmers' College) in Cincinnati, and graduated from Miami University in Oxford, Ohio, in 1852. After a period of study at a law firm Harrison was admitted to the bar in 1854. His father, John Scott Harrison, was elected a Whig congressman in 1853 and soon advised his son against politics. Harrison ignored his father, however, and campaigned for the Republican presidential candidate, John C. Frémont, in Indianapolis in 1856. He was appointed city attorney of Indianapolis in 1857 and acted as secretary of the Republican's state central committee in 1858 before becoming reporter for Indiana's supreme court in 1860, a position to which he was twice reelected.

Following the outbreak of the Civil War Harrison raised the 70th Indiana Regiment in 1862 and served as its colonel. Seeing action at Resaca, Golgotha, and New Hope Church, after his conspicuous bravery at Peach Tree Creek Harrison was promoted to brigadier general in 1865. On the cessation of hostilities Harrison returned to Indianapolis, where he practiced law, failed to be elected governor of Indiana in 1876, and served on the Mississippi River Commission between 1879 and 1881. Following his father to Congress, he became a United States senator in 1881 (refusing an offer to join Garfield's cabinet in order to do so), where he was widely acclaimed for his castigation of Cleveland's veto of veterans' pensions, but lost his seat in 1887 as a result of the opposition of Indiana's Democratic legislature.

By the time of the 1888 presidential election the free-trade-advocating Cleveland had lost the confidence of the Democrats and Harrison was able to capitalize on the disunity of the rival party, campaigning on a protectionist, "soldiers' friend" platform. Winning on the electoral, rather than the popular, vote, Harrison was inaugurated 100 years after Washington and was therefore often called the "Centennial President."

During his administration Harrison assiduously promoted high tariffs and in 1890 presided over the institution of the controversial McKinley Tariff Act, as well as the unpopular Sherman Silver Purchase Act of 1890 that increased silver coinage, the Sherman Antitrust Act of 1890 that outlawed monopolies and trusts that hampered trade, and the Dependent Pension Act that provided for Civil War veterans. All of these measures were protectionist and placed a heavy burden on the economy. When the Democrats regained control of Congress in 1890 they accordingly attacked Harrison's million-dollar national budget, to which he responded: "This is a billion-dollar country."

In conducting his foreign policy Harrison promoted U.S. interests and settled long-standing quarrels with Britain and Germany over fur seals in the Bering Sea, as well as Samoa, while the Pan-American Conference of 1889 led to mutually beneficial trade agreements with Latin America. He failed, however, to annex Hawaii.

Defeated in the presidential election of 1892 by his predecessor, Cleveland—mainly as a result of his unpopular economic measures—Harrison retired to Indianapolis, where he practiced law until his death in 1901.

Benjamin Harrison, later the 23rd president of the United States, portrayed in his uniform as an officer in the Union Army.
Elected in 1888, Harrison was the grandson of William Henry Harrison, the ninth president of the United States.

25.

WILLIAM McKINLEY (b.1843, d.1901)

Republican. President 1897–1901

Vice presidents: Garret A. Hobart, Theodore Roosevelt

William McKinley led the United States into the 20th century on a wave of triumphalism: he had defeated Spain and made the U.S.A. a world power. Only six months into his second term, however, an assassin's bullet brought the life of the 25th president to a premature end.

McKinley was born into an underprivileged household in Niles, Ohio, in 1843. He attended Allegheny College between 1860 and 1861 before illness curtailed his education. Enlisting as a private in the 23rd Ohio Volunteer Infantry on the outbreak of the Civil War, by the war's end McKinley had risen to the rank of brevet major and had served as an aide to Rutherford B. Hayes. On his return to Ohio he studied law and was admitted to the Ohio bar, later being appointed prosecuting attorney of Stark County. At the same time he played a prominent part in supporting Hayes' political aspirations (Hayes was elected president in 1876).

Voted to Congress as a Republican in 1876, apart from a year's break from 1884 to 1885 (when he lost an election), McKinley remained a member of the House of Representatives until 1891, when he was gerrymandered out of office. As a congressman McKinley spoke out in favor of tariff protection and served as chairman of the Ways and Means Committee, giving his name to the protectionist McKinley Tariff Act of 1890, which he sponsored, and which brought him national renown.

He was twice elected governor of Ohio (in 1891 and 1893) and unsuccessfully sought the Republican presidential nomination in 1892. As a result of the capable "front-porch" campaign, which was managed by the industrialist Marcus A. Hanna, "Bill McKinley and the McKinley Bill" were, however, successful against the pro-free-coinage Democrat, William J. Bryan, in the presidential election of 1896, and McKinley was inaugurated in 1897.

McKinley had vowed to continue the protectionist policies of Benjamin Harrison, particularly with regard to tariffs and supporting the gold standard, and while the Dingley Tariff of 1897 and Gold Standard Act of 1900 indeed fulfilled his promise his first administration was dominated by foreign-policy issues. Popular feeling had long supported U.S. intervention in the Cuban revolt against Spanish rule, and in 1898 matters came to a head. McKinley would have preferred to have negotiated a diplomatic solution, but was forced to request a declaration of war from Congress when Spain was accused of sinking the American ship, U.S.S. *Maine*, in Havana Harbor. The combined power of the United States Navy and Army subdued Spain within only five months, and by the Treaty of Paris of 1899 which concluded the Spanish–American War Spain ceded Guam, Puerto Rico, and the Philippines to the United States, and also gave Cuba its independence. In 1899 McKinley annexed Hawaii and Samoa and occupied Wake Island. In addition, by sending a U.S. force of 5,000 to China during the Boxer Rebellion, McKinley signaled America's newly won status as a world power.

The victory over Spain was an important factor in McKinley's reelection in 1900, and he now prepared to concentrate on domestic policy. On September 6, 1901, however, he was shot by a Polish anarchist, Leon Czolgosz, at the Pan-American Exposition in Buffalo, New York. The fatally wounded McKinley died eight days later.

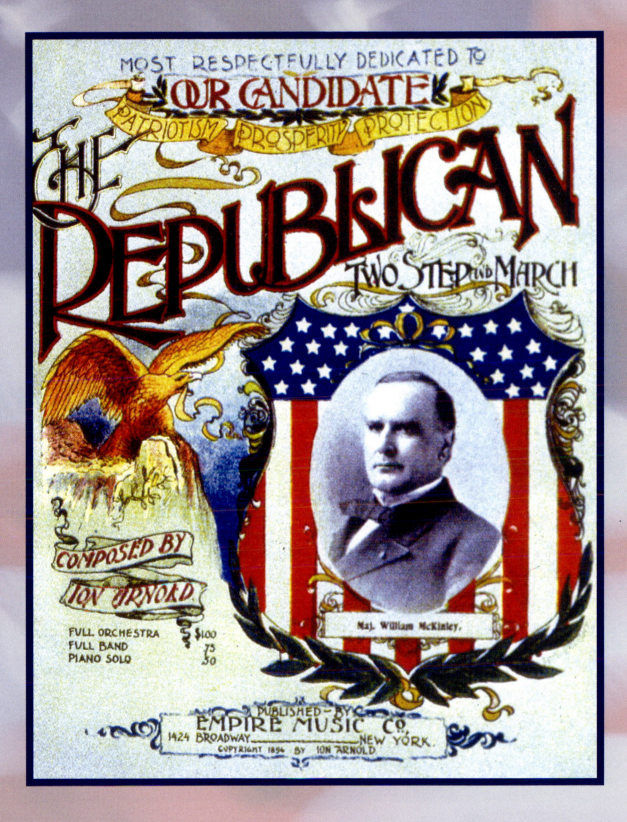

The cover of the sheet music to the "Republican Two-Step and March," composed in honor of the Republican presidential candidate William McKinley.

President William McKinley makes an address to the people. McKinley won the elections of 1896 and 1900, but was assassinated in Buffalo, New York, in 1901.

William McKinley, the 25th president of the United States, pictured on the porch of his home in Canton, Ohio. During the 1896 election McKinley campaigned from his porch while his opponent, William Jennings Bryan, toured the country.

THEODORE ROOSEVELT (b.1858, d.1919)

Republican. President 1901–1909

Vice president: Charles W. Fairbanks

The assassination of McKinley may have made Theodore Roosevelt president by default, but he proved to be one of America's most dynamic leaders. Although he served two swashbuckling terms and received the Nobel Peace Prize, more prosaically, his name has been immortalized by a cuddly toy: the "teddy" bear.

Roosevelt was born in 1858, in New York City, into a prominent banking family. Despite his asthma and astigmatism, the young Roosevelt built up his strength with energetic pursuits. He graduated from Harvard in 1880 and was elected to the New York state assembly in 1881 as a Republican. In 1884 the double tragedy of the death of his wife and mother caused Roosevelt to resign his seat and to settle in Dakota Territory, where he worked as a cattle rancher until 1886.

After his remarriage Roosevelt's interest in politics resurfaced, and he became variously a corruption-hating member of the Civil Service Commission in 1889, president of the Police Commission in New York City in 1895, and, in 1897, assistant secretary of the navy in McKinley's first administration. Unlike the more cautious McKinley, Roosevelt was an enthusiastic supporter of war with Spain over Cuba, and on the outbreak of hostilities in 1898 resigned his position in order to participate in the fighting. After raising the 1st Volunteer Cavalry Regiment (the "Rough Riders"), Colonel Roosevelt was fêted for leading a charge up Kettle Hill during the battle for San Juan.

Following the war's conclusion, the war hero Roosevelt was elected governor of New York State in 1898, but he exasperated many Republicans with his reforming policies; his nomination as McKinley's vice president in 1900 was primarily designed to remove him to what was perceived to be a less damaging position. The following year, however, "madman" Roosevelt was sworn in as president.

The new president soon earned a reputation for "carrying a big stick." In domestic affairs, the "Trust Buster" demonstrated his determination to regulate trusts (he indicted 25), and to prevent economic monopolies: in 1902 he instituted proceedings against the Northern Security Company, resulting in its dissolution by the Supreme Court in 1904. Preferring regulated capitalism to *laissez-faire*, Roosevelt's threat to bring in federal troops to operate mines during the United Mine Workers' strike in Pennsylvania in 1902 forced a settlement. Roosevelt was no less forceful in his foreign policy: when his attempt to purchase the rights to build a canal in Colombia was rejected in 1903 Roosevelt supported a revolution against the Colombian government, thereby securing his canal in Panama. The Roosevelt Corollary furthermore extended the Monroe Doctrine.

Roosevelt was reelected in 1904 with a huge majority. During his second term in office he was responsible for instigating the "Square Deal" regulatory legislation of 1906, including the Hepburn Act for railroads, the Meat Inspection Act, and the Pure Food and Drug Act, as well as measures for doubling the number of national parks. In 1905, as a result of his mediation following the Russo–Japanese War, he became the first U.S. winner of the Nobel Peace Prize; somewhat inappropriately, in 1907 the Nobel laureate sent the "Great White Fleet" of 16 battleships around the world to show off the U.S.A.'s might.

Roosevelt retired in 1909, leaving the presidency in the hands of his protégé, William H. Taft, but by the time of the presidential election of 1912 he had become dissatisfied with Taft's performance and allowed himself to be renominated. When he failed to be confirmed (as a result of the conservatives' fear of his brand of progressive Republicanism), he stood as candidate of his own, "Bull Moose" Progressive Party, but in splitting the vote lost to Democrat Woodrow Wilson, whom Roosevelt later denounced for his delay in entering World War I. Robust to the last, he died in 1919.

President Theodore Roosevelt, who succeeded William McKinley after his assassination, was a popular leader
and the first American to receive the Nobel Peace Prize, which was awarded for his mediation in the Russo–Japanese War.
In the election of 1912 Roosevelt ran for president as the candidate of the Progressive Party.

Theodore Roosevelt, later the 26th president of the United States, riding out with the volunteer cavalry regiment known as the "Rough Riders." His company took part in the famous Battle of San Juan Hill in Cuba during the Spanish–American War.

Theodore Roosevelt on a hunting tour in central Africa.

27.

WILLIAM H. TAFT (b.1857, d.1930)

Republican. President 1909–1913

Vice president: James S. Sherman

William H. Taft was groomed for the presidency by Roosevelt himself, but proved to be a less than worthy successor to the charismatic "T.R." Recalled from retirement in 1921, Taft was more effective in his subsequent capacity as chief justice, and is the only American to have held both the United States' highest executive and judicial offices.

On his birth in 1857, in Cincinnati, Ohio, the young Taft—whose grandfather had been a judge and whose father, Alphonso, had served as secretary of war, attorney general, and ambassador to Austria-Hungary, as well as Russia—seemed destined for a judicial career. After attending Yale, from which he graduated in 1878, he was awarded a law degree from the Cincinnati Law School in 1880 and was later admitted to the bar. After setting up his own legal practice Taft served as assistant prosecuting attorney of Hamilton County between 1881 and 1883 and as collector of internal revenue for Cincinnati in 1882; in 1888 he was elected to the Ohio superior court. Appointed U.S. solicitor general in 1890, in 1892 he was named circuit judge for Washington's sixth district.

Although a Republican sympathizer, Taft would undoubtedly have preferred quietly to advance his judicial career, but his wife harbored political ambitions on his behalf. As civil governor of the Philippines between 1900 and 1904 Taft displayed impressive impartiality, and his governorship was a highpoint of his career. Indeed, on Roosevelt's election as president his old friend twice offered Taft a place on the Supreme Court, which Taft rejected so that he could continue his administration of the Philippines. Eventually, however, he accepted the position of secretary of war, and, as such, gained a reputation as a skilled mediator.

When the phenomenally popular Roosevelt declined a third term the reluctant Taft was unable to withstand pressure from both Roosevelt and his family to stand for election as the Republican candidate in the presidential election of 1908. He was swept into office on a tide of Roosevelt's reflected glory and promised to continue his predecessor's reforms. Although Taft created the Tariff Board to investigate tariffs and enforced the Sherman Antitrust Act, the Payne-Aldrich Act of 1909 lowered the tariff, thereby alienating many. Less controversially, under his presidency the parcel-post and the postal-savings systems were set up, while Arizona and New Mexico were admitted to the United States. During his administration, too, provisions were made for a federal income tax and for senators to be voted into office directly.

To the progressive wing of the Republican Party, it seemed that the passive Taft had watered down, if not betrayed, Roosevelt's policies, and in 1912 Taft found himself facing his predecessor in the race for the Republican presidential nomination. Taft was the conservative choice, however, and Roosevelt was defeated. In putting himself forward as an independent, Progressive candidate, Roosevelt subsequently succeeded only in splitting the Republican vote, with the result that the Democrat Woodrow Wilson was elected president.

Taft retired with some relief to become professor of law at Yale and served as joint chairman of the National War Labor Board during World War I. In recognition of his outstanding expertise in the judicial field, President Warren Harding recalled Taft in 1921, appointing him chief justice of the Supreme Court. Thus Taft began nearly a decade of happy and successful service, during which he was notable for reorganizing the Supreme Court and also for increasing its speed of work. Forced to resign because of ill health in 1930, Taft died a few months later.

William Howard Taft, the 27th U.S. president, had a distinguished judicial career.

28.

WOODROW WILSON (b.1856, d.1924)

Democrat. President 1913–1921

Vice president: Thomas R. Marshall

The period of Woodrow Wilson's presidency was a time of reform and turbulence, during which the United States entered World War I and emerged victorious. A Nobel laureate, Wilson is also remembered as the inspiration behind the League of Nations.

Born in 1856 in Staunton, Virginia, the son of a Presbyterian minister who served as a Confederate chaplain, as a child Wilson witnessed the horrors of the Civil War at first hand. After his graduation from the College of New Jersey (now Princeton University) in 1879, illness curtailed his attendance at the University of Virginia's Law School in 1880, but in 1882 he was admitted to the bar and opened his own law firm. Abandoning the struggle to drum up work, Wilson resumed his academic studies at John Hopkins University, receiving his doctorate in political studies in 1886. After teaching at the Bryn Mawr and Wesleyan colleges, in 1890 Wilson was appointed professor of jurisprudence at Princeton and became its president in 1902. He remained in this position until 1910, when, demoralized by criticism of his attempts to reform and democratize the university, he resigned. Voted governor of New Jersey, between 1911 and 1913 Wilson became known as a radical Democratic reformer.

Following his nomination as Democratic presidential candidate on the 46th ballot Wilson benefited from the divisions in the Republican Party and was elected president in 1912, promising "New Freedom." During his first term Wilson pushed through the Underwood Tariff Act of 1913 which removed tariffs from exports, lowered rates on imports, and introduced income tax. The Federal Reserve Act was passed in 1913, and the Federal Trade Commission was created in 1914, while with the Clayton Antitrust Act of 1914 labor unions were legalized. In the pursuance of an unexpectedly vigorous foreign policy, Wilson ordered the occupation of Veracruz in 1914 in order to encourage the unseating of the murderous Mexican president, Huerta, and sent General Pershing into Mexican territory in 1916 to suppress the bandit rebel Pancho Villa.

Wilson's presidency was unquestionably dominated by World War I. Wilson—a convinced pacifist—was initially disinclined to involve the United States in what seemed to be essentially a European matter. He accordingly proclaimed the U.S.A.'s neutrality and, despite the severe provocation of the German sinking of the British liner *Lusitania*, causing the death of 100 Americans, adhered to this position until 1917. When, in 1916, Wilson campaigned under the slogan "He kept us out of war," he was elected to serve a second term. The aggressive attacks of German submarines against U.S. merchant shipping intensified, however, until in 1917 Woodrow was compelled to request Congress to declare war on Germany in order to "make the world safe for democracy." Although the U.S. entry into World War I was late, it proved decisive, and the armistice of November 11, 1918 ended the Great War.

Wilson was determined to prevent the recurrence of future such wars, and as early as January 1918 had outlined his Fourteen Points for peace, which included provision for a league of nations. The Treaty of Versailles of 1919 was distressingly punitive from Wilson's point of view, but at least it endorsed a league of nations. He returned to the United States with the task of obtaining the treaty's ratification by the Senate and embarked on a nationwide tour in 1919 to encourage its support. During the tour, however, he suffered a stroke, from then on being virtually incapacitated, although he served out his term of office. In 1920, the year in which Wilson was awarded the Nobel Peace Prize, the Senate rejected the Treaty of Versailles and the Republican candidate, Warren Harding, won the presidential election. Wilson died in 1924.

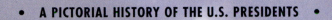

Woodrow Wilson, the 28th president of the United States, was a pacifist who took the U.S.A into World War I.

29.
WARREN G. HARDING (b.1865, d.1923)

Republican. President 1921–1923

Vice president: Calvin Coolidge

During the postwar presidential-election campaign of 1920 Warren Harding promised a return to "normalcy." Yet his administration proved anything but normal and was finally completely discredited by scandal. Harding himself was weak rather than corrupt and certainly acted with an amazing lack of foresight or prudence. Woodrow Wilson commented that he possessed a "bungalow mind," and, indeed, Harding once observed "I know how far removed from greatness I am."

The first journalist to become U.S. president, Harding was born into a farming family in Blooming Grove, Corsica, Ohio, in 1865. He graduated from Ohio Central College in 1882, the same year in which the Hardings moved to Marion. After a single term of teaching school he flirted with the law and sold insurance. Turning to journalism in 1884, he was sacked from the *Marion Mirror* for his enthusiasm for the Republican presidential candidate James G. Blaine. Harding, however, had been bitten by the journalistic bug, and along with two partners acquired the ailing *Marion Star*. Contrary to the expectations of many, the newspaper became a success.

Harding's geniality and talent for oratory helped him to become elected a Republican member of the Ohio senate in 1899, in which he served a second term before being voted lieutenant governor in 1902—largely as the result of the support of Harry M. Daugherty. After his failure to be elected governor in 1910 he was elected to the U. S. Senate in 1914, where he spent six convivial, but politically uneventful, years.

In 1917 Harding endeared himself to Roosevelt by sponsoring a bill that, if passed, would have allowed Roosevelt to raise a volunteer army to serve in World War I, and in 1919 the appreciative Roosevelt proposed Harding as his running mate in the 1920 election. Roosevelt died before the election took place, but—as a result of Daugherty's efforts—on the tenth ballot Harding was nominated the Republican candidate for the presidency and campaigned on a "return to normalcy" ticket. The war-weary U.S. public responded and Harding was elected president in an overwhelming victory over the Democrat James M. Cox.

Unlike many of his more vigorous predecessors, Harding was a passive, conservative Republican, who believed that Congress, rather than the president, should instigate legislation. As the proponent of "less government in business, more business in government," he created the Bureau of the Budget and approved the Fordney-McCumber Tariff Act of 1922, but generally preferred a policy of *laissez-faire* to one of economic control. Rather than administrating, Harding was happier to play poker and drink (despite Prohibition) with his cronies, or to visit his mistresses. Furthermore, although he made some sensible appointments, he unwisely promoted members of the "Ohio Gang" (including Daugherty as attorney general) to positions of prominence. Along with the increasing economic depression, by 1923 a series of brewing scandals regarding abuses in Daugherty's Department of Justice and Charles R. Forbes Veterans' Bureau—among others—were threatening to blow apart Harding's administration.

In 1923 Harding was on a nationwide tour—the "Voyage of Understanding"—to promote the U.S.A.'s joining of the World Court when he received word that the transgressions of members of his administration were about to be exposed. He immediately fell ill and died a few months later. He was publicly mourned—that is, until the "Teapot Dome" scandal, which involved bribery over oil reserves, implicated Daugherty, Albert B. Fall, and Forbes shortly afterward. Fall and Forbes were jailed, but Daugherty escaped with dismissal.

Warren Gamaliel Harding, the U.S.A.'s 29th president.

30.

CALVIN COOLIDGE (b.1872, d.1933)

Republican. President 1923–1929

Vice president: Charles G. Dawes

After the scandal-rocked administration of the convivial Warren G. Harding, perhaps it was the stark contrast of the undeniably dull Calvin Coolidge that made the 30th president such a popular figure. Certainly he appeared to have brought political stability and dramatic economic growth to the United States during the heady years of the Roaring Twenties, although in the following decade his policies became largely discredited.

Appropriately enough, given his presidential destiny, Coolidge was born on Independence Day, 1872, in Plymouth Notch, Vermont. He was the first of his family to receive further education, and after graduating from Amherst College in 1895 studied and clerked for the Northampton, Massachusetts, law firm of John Hammond and Henry Field. He was admitted to the bar in 1897 and subsequently set up a thriving legal practice in Northampton. Encouraged by the Republican Hammond and Field, Coolidge developed an interest in politics. He served as city councillor in 1898, and then as city solicitor, before being voted mayor of Northampton in both 1909 and 1910. Coolidge was elected a Republican state senator in 1911 and after having been voted president of the senate in 1913 his firm leadership was acknowledged by his appointment to the position of lieutenant governor in 1915. In 1918 he was elected governor of Massachusetts and was widely applauded for his handling of the Boston Police Strike of 1919, when he assumed command of the state guard and denied the strikers' right to return to their jobs, justifying his actions with the reproof: "There is no right to strike against the public safety by anybody, anywhere, any time."

Coolidge's dramatic suppression of the strike not only won him reelection as governor, but also brought him to national prominence, and in 1920 he won the Republican Party's nomination as vice president to Harding's president. On hearing of Harding's death after only two years as president, Coolidge was sworn into office by his father in Plymouth Notch. By dying before news of it broke Harding had escaped the aftermath of the "Tea Dome" scandal of 1923, and it was left to Coolidge to try to restore national confidence in the presidency; he did so by dismissing and prosecuting those involved. Having won respect for his uncompromising actions, as well as for his undoubted integrity, Coolidge now presided over a "clean" administration.

By 1924 Coolidge had been so successful in rehabilitating the reputation of the presidency that he was elected president in his own right in a resounding victory. His second term in office was marked by the restoration of diplomatic contact with Mexico and by the multilateral Kellogg-Briand Pact of 1928, which renounced war in favor of negotiation. Recognizing the impossibly high level of German war reparations, Coolidge furthermore helped to alleviate this burden by means of the Dawes Plan. Domestically, Coolidge reduced taxes, as well as the national debt, thus freeing more money for consumer spending. This was entirely in accordance with his conservative Republican, *laissez-faire*, anti-interventionist attitude, and was welcomed while the U.S. economy boomed, but would later result in the Wall Street Crash of 1929 and the subsequent Great Depression.

Toward the end of his second term Coolidge appeared to have lost his appetite for politics and announced in 1927 "I do not choose to run for president in 1928." Despite his popularity, "Silent Cal" remained true to his word and retired to Northampton, where he lived quietly until his death in 1933.

Calvin Coolidge, the 30th U.S. president, cleaned up the Republican administration.

31.

HERBERT HOOVER (b.1874, d.1964)

Republican. President 1929–1933

Vice president: Charles Curtis

The presidency of Herbert Hoover may have directly followed that of his fellow-Republican Calvin Coolidge, but the issues that each man faced could hardly have been more different. For while the 30th president presided over a period of economic boom, the administration of the 31st was bedeviled by the worst years of the Great Depression.

Born in 1874, into a Quaker family in West Branch, Iowa, Hoover was left an orphan at the age of nine and subsequently lived with an uncle in Oregon. He graduated in mine engineering from Stanford University in 1895 and worked in the mines of California and Colorado before joining a San Francisco firm of engineers. In 1897 Hoover became chief of mining for the British firm Bewick, Moreing, and Company, in Western Australia, after which he was appointed chief engineer of the Chinese Engineering and Mining Company in 1898. The Boxer Rebellion of 1900 saw Hoover taking the lead in the distribution of food to the besieged foreign community of Tientsin.

In 1901 Hoover rejoined Bewick, Moreing, and Company as a junior partner and traveled the world before setting up his own consultative engineering firm in 1908, whose spectacular success soon made him a millionaire. Finding himself in London on the outbreak of World War I, Hoover established the American Relief Committee to help Americans in Europe to return home. Drawing upon his experience in China, he furthermore established the Commission for Relief in German-occupied Belgium and northern France in 1915, which would succor ten million people. When the United States entered the hostilities in 1917 Hoover was appointed head of the United States Food Administration Department, where his "wheatless" and "meatless" days resulted in the verb "to Hooverize" becoming synonymous with being economical with food. Recognizing his outstanding abilities in this field, in 1918 the Allies appointed Hoover director of relief and rehabilitation for Europe, while his American Relief Administration worked to alleviate the suffering of millions.

Appointed secretary of commerce in 1921, Hoover served in this capacity under both Harding and Coolidge, capably coordinating various manufacturing concerns. He was subsequently nominated the Republican presidential candidate upon Coolidge's retirement, promising "a chicken in every pot, a car in every garage." Riding the contemporary wave of economic prosperity, Hoover won a convincing victory over the Democrat Al Smith and was duly elected president in 1928.

The stock-market crash of October 29, 1929 ended the boom years and heralded profound economic depression. Despite his leadership of voluntary industrial emergency conferences it soon became clear that Hoover's policy of nonintervention was doomed to failure. By 1932 nearly 14 million Americans were unemployed (the collections of shacks that housed them were disparagingly termed "Hoovervilles"), and the president's popularity suffered proportionately. The crisis came when an army of World War I veterans marched on Washington in 1932 to demand the early distribution of war bonds. Despite the agreement of the House of Representatives, the Senate's refusal prompted rioting and Hoover ordered federal troops to disperse the "Bonus" campaigners. This heavy-handed response was widely criticized, and despite the more positive establishment of the Reconstruction Finance Corporation in 1932 was instrumental in Hoover's defeat by Franklin D. Roosevelt in the presidential election of that year.

Hoover retired to California, where he wrote extensively and also traveled the world to attempt to help to avert famine after World War II. Between 1947 and 1955 the "Hoover Commissions" which he headed furthermore reorganized the executive branch of government. Variously tagged the "Great Engineer," the "Great Humanitarian," the "Great Secretary," and the "Great Public Servant" (but tellingly not the "Great President"), Hoover died in 1964.

Herbert Hoover, the 31st U.S. president, was termed the "Great Humanitarian," but not the "Great President."

32.

FRANKLIN DELANO ROOSEVELT
(b.1882, d.1945)

Democrat. President 1933–1945

Vice presidents: John N. Garner, Henry A. Wallace, Harry S. Truman

The charismatic U.S. president, Franklin Delano Roosevelt was elected for an unprecedented four terms, but then the circumstances of his presidency—the deepest economic depression and bitterest world war to date—were also unusual, and "F.D.R." himself was an extraordinary, if controversial, man.

Born in 1882, in Hyde Park, New York, the only child of a wealthy railroad executive, Roosevelt's background was one of privilege. After being privately educated at home and at Groton School Roosevelt graduated from Harvard in 1903 before studying at the Columbia University Law School. After passing his state bar exams, he left law school without a degree and joined a New York law firm. In 1905 he married a distant cousin, Eleanor Roosevelt—the niece of President Theodore Roosevelt—who would later become one of the U.S.A.'s most celebrated first ladies.

Roosevelt entered politics in 1910, when, as a Democrat, he won a Republican seat on the New York senate, and came to prominence in 1912, when he supported the presidential candidacy of Woodrow Wilson against that of his fifth cousin, "T.R." After Wilson's election F.D.R. was rewarded with the position of assistant secretary of the navy in 1913. Along with his undoubted capability, his well-publicized visits to the battlefields of Europe during World War I brought Roosevelt national renown and he was nominated Democratic vice president to James M. Cox in 1920, only to be defeated by the Republican Harding-Coolidge team. The following year, Roosevelt was struck down with polio and became paralyzed; he later mastered his affliction with the help of crutches and leg braces.

Following his election as governor of New York state in 1928, and his subsequent reelection in 1930, Roosevelt's progressive, depression-beating policies (as well as his "fireside chats" on the radio) made him the ideal presidential candidate for both the Democratic Party and the "forgotten man." He defeated Hoover in the election of 1932 with a platform that promised to bring an end to the Depression by means of "New Deal" policies, and during the course of 100 days subsequently instigated an "alphabet soup" of agencies, such as the T.V.A. (the Tennessee Valley Authority, whose dams produced cheap electricity), and programs with which to accomplish this goal. Although controversial, his policies were effective, and measures such as the deflationary Economy Act, the reform of the currency and banks, the regulation of the stock market by the Securities and Exchange Commission, as well as welfare relief and aid to struggling farmers and industries, helped to reelect Roosevelt in 1936.

His second term was dominated by the outbreak of World War II in 1939. Like Wilson before him, Roosevelt appeared reluctant to involve the United States in a European war, and this popular stance resulted in a further victory in the presidential election of 1940, giving him an unprecedented third term. Despite his theoretical neutrality, Roosevelt was markedly sympathetic to the Allies, his Lend-Lease program, for example, supplying them with U.S. weapons. In December 1941, however, the Japanese attacked the U.S. Navy at Pearl Harbor, thus precipitating the United States' entry into the war against the Axis powers. During the course of the hostilities Roosevelt proved himself an outstanding strategist and diplomat. After the D-Day landings of June 1944 it appeared that the Allies would defeat Hitler and Roosevelt was reelected in November with a mandate to complete the task.

Shortly before the war's end, in February 1945, Roosevelt met Churchill and Stalin at Yalta, but he was clearly already exhausted. Roosevelt died in April 1945, to universal desolation. It was left to Truman to conclude the peace.

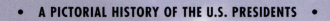

U.S. president Franklin D. Roosevelt photographed after proclaiming a state of "unlimited national emergency" during World War II.

PICTURE POST

Franklin D. Roosevelt (*right*) and his vice president and successor Harry Truman.

Left: Franklin Delano Roosevelt, president of the United States from 1933 to 1945, was elected during the Great Depression and presided over the nation's economic recovery, which was accomplished through a program of legislative reform known as the "New Deal." He led the nation during World War II, issuing a declaration of war on Japan in 1941 and attending the Allied conferences at Tehran and Yalta. Roosevelt was the only president to be elected for four consecutive terms.

33.

HARRY S. TRUMAN (b.1884, d.1972)

Democrat. President 1945–1953

Vice president: Albert W. Barkley

After his unexpected elevation to the presidency in April 1945, it was Harry S. Truman who oversaw the surrender of Germany, and on whose orders the atomic bombs that ended the war with Japan were dropped. In the uneasy aftermath of World War II it was also Truman who shaped the American anticommunist stance of the Cold War years.

Truman was born into a farming family in Lamar, Missouri, in 1884. Myopia dashed his dream of entering West Point; instead he held down a variety of jobs and between 1906 and 1917 helped to run the family farm. Following the U.S.A.'s entry into World War I in 1917, Captain Truman commanded Battery D of the 129th Field Artillery in France. At the end of the war Truman opened a haberdashery store in Kansas City; the venture failed in 1922 however, and he spent the next 15 years paying off huge debts.

Deciding that business was clearly not for him, Truman developed an interest in politics and gained the support of "Big Tom" Prendergast, the leader of Kansas City's Democrats. He was voted a county judge in 1922 (more an administrative than a legal position) and subsequently served as presiding county judge between 1926 and 1934. With the help of Prendergast, he was elected to the United States Senate in 1934 and despite the influential Prendergast's imprisonment for tax evasion was reelected in 1940. As head of the Committee to Investigate the National Defense Program (the "Truman Committee") from 1941, Truman's efficiency saved the nation $15 billion, and his popularity resulted in his nomination as Roosevelt's vice president in 1944.

President Roosevelt died in April 1945—a month before Germany's surrender—and Truman stepped into his shoes with some trepidation; one of his first acts was attending the founding conference of the United Nations. In July 1945 Truman was faced with the difficult moral decision of authorizing the dropping of atomic bombs on Hiroshima and Nagasaki; although controversial, the resulting nuclear devastation prompted Japan's surrender in August.

Stalin's motives had aroused Truman's distrust at Potsdam in 1945, and the U.S.S.R.'s subsequent expansion into Eastern Europe seemed to confirm the Soviet danger. In 1947 the Truman Doctrine therefore pronounced the United States' determination to "support free peoples who are resisting attempted subjugation"—effectively to fight communism worldwide—thus signaling an end to the U.S.A.'s traditional peacetime isolationism. Truman also sponsored the Marshall Plan to provide aid for the economic reconstruction of Europe and recognized the state of Israel in 1948.

In his domestic policy Truman initiated the "Fair Deal" program of social reform, but in doing so faced concerted Republican opposition. Despite the skeptics' belief that the Democrats could not win the presidential election of 1948 against the strong Republican challenge of Thomas Dewey, "Give 'Em Hell Harry" Truman was reelected president. While his first presidency had been marked by immediate postwar issues, his second was dominated by the outbreak of the Korean War in 1950. In accordance with the Truman Doctrine the president committed the United States to preventing the subjugation of South Korea by the communist North Korea, but in 1951 removed General MacArthur from his position of United Nations commander when the latter advocated an extension of the war into China. In 1949 the United States joined N.A.T.O., and in 1950 Truman's Four Point Program announced the funding of underdeveloped nations.

By 1952, with negotiations to end the Korean War still dragging on, Truman had decided against seeking renomination and retired to Missouri. Here the "little man" who had risen to greatness lived an active life until his death in 1972.

The Truman Doctrine—January 1, 1947
U.S. president Harry S. Truman pictured signing the Foreign Aid Assistance Act, which provided a program of foreign aid to Greece and Turkey.
The provision of economic support to any nation resisting communist pressure came to be known as the Truman Doctrine.

34.

DWIGHT D. EISENHOWER (b.1890, d.1969)

Republican. President 1953–1961

Vice president: Richard M. Nixon

Dwight D. Eisenhower's resounding success as Allied supreme commander during World War II may have prompted his election to the presidency, but behind the military glory lay real substance.

Eisenhower was born in 1890, in Denison, Texas, but when he was two his family moved to Abilene, Kansas. Despite his fundamentalist-Christian parents' deeply held pacifism, they allowed their son to enter West Point in 1911, from which he graduated in 1915. Following a posting to Texas, after the U.S.A's entry into World War I Captain Eisenhower ran a tank-training program in Gettysburg, Pennsylvania. Study at tank school and a posting to the Panama Canal Zone followed. In 1926 he graduated (first in his class) from the Command and General Staff School, and in 1928 from the Army War College. Between 1929 and 1933 he worked in the office of the assistant secretary of war before being appointed aide to Douglas MacArthur, the chief of staff, in 1933.

By 1941 Eisenhower was a brigadier general. The Japanese attack on Pearl Harbor, and the United States' subsequent declaration of war on the Axis powers, resulted in his posting to the War Plans Division, where he gained notice but continued to chafe at being deskbound. Chief of Staff Marshall, however, recognized Eisenhower's potential, and after creating him head of the Operations Division in July 1942 sent him to London as commanding general of the U.S. forces in the European theater, in which capacity he successfully directed the landings in North Africa in 1942 and the invasions of Sicily and Italy in 1943. In recognition of his abilities, in December 1943 Eisenhower was given the unprecedented title of Supreme Commander of the Allied Expeditionary Force and threw his energy into planning the D-Day landings of June 6, 1944. The ultimate Allied victory was in no small part due to Eisenhower's skills as a tactician, as well as his diplomacy in uniting the Allied generals under his command.

Returning to the United States to a hero's welcome, Eisenhower settled into his peacetime role as the army's chief of staff, but retired in 1949 to serve as president of Columbia University; in 1950 he was appointed the first supreme commander of N.A.T.O. In 1952, however, having been wooed by both the Republican and Democratic parties, Eisenhower resigned from the army and stood as the Republican candidate for the presidency, beating Adlai E. Stevenson comprehensively.

Having vowed "I shall go to Korea," Eisenhower immediately did so, and presided over a truce to end the war in 1953. Eisenhower's talents as a strategist and administrator had been proved beyond doubt during World War II. While his "modern Republicanism" policies continued the social programs of his Democratic predecessors, Eisenhower also championed public-works initiatives, such as the development of the interstate highway system, and eventually balanced the national budget. Controversially, however, he did little actively to oppose the anticommunist McCarthy witch-hunts.

During Eisenhower's first administration the U.S.A.'s economy was booming, and his reelection in 1956 was virtually a foregone conclusion. Between 1957 and 1958, however, the economy was in recession, and Eisenhower was being confronted with difficulties both at home and abroad. When the Soviets shot down a U.S. U-2 spy plane in 1960, U.S. relations with the U.S.S.R. reached a low point. In 1961, after Castro had seized U.S. property in Cuba, Eisenhower furthermore terminated diplomatic relations with that country. At home, racial integration was being hotly debated, and Eisenhower controversially sent federal troops to Little Rock, Arkansas, in 1957 to enforce the desegregation of its high school.

Eisenhower retired in 1961 to Gettysburg. He suffered a heart attack in 1965 and died in 1969, with his popularity undiminished.

Dwight D. Eisenhower, Supreme Commander of the Allied Expeditionary Force and 34th president of the U.S.A.

Former U.S. general and 34th U.S. president Dwight D. Eisenhower.

Right: Dwight D. Eisenhower, who was affectionately known as "Ike," pictured with his wife Mamie.

35.

JOHN F. KENNEDY (b.1917, d.1963)

Democrat. President 1961–1963

Vice president: Lyndon B. Johnson

Although John F. Kennedy was by no means the first president to be assassinated while still in office, his death was a defining moment in U.S. history. He is remembered as the youthful and glamorous leader of "Camelot," who successfully confronted the Soviet Union and carried the nation's hopes with him.

Kennedy was born in Brookline, Massachusetts, in 1917, the second son of Rose and Joseph Kennedy. His father harbored the highest ambitions for his sons and groomed both Joseph and John (or "Jack") for high office. Kennedy studied at the London School of Economics in 1935, but his subsequent attendance at Princeton was curtailed by illness. Following his graduation from Harvard, Kennedy's thesis regarding the causes of World War II was published in 1940 as the acclaimed *Why England Slept*. During the early 1940s he studied at the Stanford University Graduate School of Business and visited Latin America before joining the navy in 1941. He was awarded a Purple Heart in 1943 for his courageous actions following the sinking of his P.T. boat by the Japanese.

After working briefly as a journalist, in 1946 Kennedy was elected to the U.S. House of Representatives as a Democrat, thus replacing Joseph (who had been killed during World War II) as the focus of his familiy's political ambitions. In 1952 he was voted to the Senate, winning the seat of the Republican senator Henry Cabot Lodge. His recurring back injury necessitated an operation, and during his convalescence between 1954 and 1955 Kennedy wrote his second book—*Profiles in Courage*—for which he won a Pulitzer Prize in 1957. Undaunted by his failure to be nominated the Democratic vice president in 1956, by 1960 Kennedy had set his sights on the presidency. A master of the media of television, whose appeal was compounded by his glamorous wife, Kennedy ran rings round the Republican Nixon and was elected the United States' youngest, and first Catholic, president.

Following his inauguration in January 1961, when he challenged Americans to "ask not what your country can do for you—ask what you can do for your country," he faced his first crisis in April 1961, with the disastrous Bay of Pigs invasion (planned during the Eisenhower era), in which C.I.A.-sponsored Cuban rebels failed to overthrow Castro. Kennedy met Khrushchev in Vienna two months later to discuss the Berlin issue, but did not impress the Soviet premier, who was determined to challenge the might of the United States. In 1962 the Soviets accordingly began to install missiles on Cuba within range of the United States. During the resulting Cuban Missile Crisis Kennedy blockaded the shipment of weapons for Cuba and demanded the missiles' removal. He was finally able to convince the Soviets that the United States would respond in kind, thereby averting the nuclear war to which the world had come perilously close. Indeed, in 1963 the Soviet–U.S. Nuclear Test Ban Treaty furthermore agreed the ending of the atmospheric testing of nuclear weapons.

Kennedy was now perceived as the leader of the "Free World," but still faced dissent at home. His planned "New Frontier" of progressive legislation included several hard-hitting civil-rights proposals, and by 1963 Kennedy was waging a continuing battle with Congress over the enactment of many measures. Less controversially, 1961 marked the founding of both the Alliance for Progress, which provided economic support to Latin America, and the Peace Corps.

On November 22, 1963, Kennedy was shot and killed in Dallas, Texas, by the Soviet sympathizer Lee Harvey Oswald (although a conspiracy was widely suspected). Kennedy's early death has since made him a figure of legend.

John F. Kennedy at a press conference in Washington D.C., September 1960.

John F. Kennedy and Jacqueline Bouvier pictured enjoying the sunshine at Kennedy's family home at Hyannis Port, Massachusetts, a few months before their wedding.

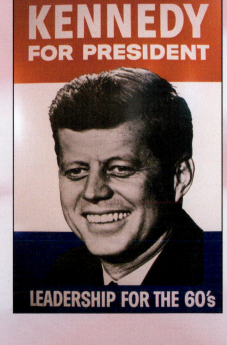

Right: A campaign poster for John F. Kennedy.

Left: President Kennedy photographed greeting a crowd of enthusiastic well-wishers in West Virginia.

36.

LYNDON B. JOHNSON (b.1908, d.1973)

Democrat. President 1963–1969

Vice president: Hubert H. Humphrey

For many, the enduring image of Lyndon B. Johnson remains his swearing-in as president on *Air Force One* following Kennedy's assassination. His administration was overshadowed by Kennedy's death, as well as by the Vietnam War, but his progressive policies have also earned him retrospective acclaim.

Born in 1908 near Stonewall, Texas, into an impoverished farming family, Johnson graduated from high school in 1924 and worked as a manual laborer before entering the Southwest Texas State Teachers College in 1927, from which he graduated in 1930. His father had served on the Texas legislature and therefore had many political connections, so after a year during which he taught school Johnson was appointed Congressional secretary to Richard M. Kleberg in Washington, D.C, where he became an adept student of the machinery of government. In 1935 he was appointed Texas administrator of the National Youth Administration, which was charged with educating and employing young people, and his popularity in this post resulted in his election to the U.S. House of Representatives as a Democrat in 1937.

Having failed to be elected to the Senate in 1941, Representative Johnson's political career was interrupted by World War II, during which he served in the Pacific as a naval lieutenant commander before being recalled to Congress in 1942. In 1948 he was at last voted to the U.S. Senate, where he soon demonstrated an outstanding understanding of legislative politics; in 1955 the minority leader of 1953 became majority leader of the Senate, which he remained until 1961. As well as consolidating his own position, as a senator Johnson furthermore fought for the Civil Rights acts of 1957 and 1960, also promoting welfare legislation.

Although he had himself hoped for the Democratic presidential nomination of 1960, Kennedy's death in November 1963 brought Vice President Johnson the presidency in the unhappiest of circumstances. He resolved to push through the program of progressive reforms that had been initiated by his predecessor, and, indeed, it was he, not Kennedy, who would help to alleviate U.S. poverty, and who would preside over the enactment of the Civil Rights bill in 1964 (which banned discrimination in public places), as well as of the Voting Rights bill of 1965. As a result, the tough advocate of a free "Great Society" was elected on his own account in a landslide victory in 1964.

Vietnam, however, doomed Johnson's second term in office. China, rather than the Soviet Union, was now perceived as representing the greatest threat to world security, and since the late 1950s a limited force of U.S. troops had been supporting South Vietnam against the Chinese-sponsored Vietcong. Following an attack on some U.S. patrol boats off Vietnam in 1964, Johnson secured Congress's approval of the Gulf of Tonkin Resolution, which granted him a free hand in Vietnam. As a result, during the following years he dramatically increased the number of U.S. "advisors" in South Vietnam and ordered the bombing of North Vietnam. By 1968 Vietnam had become a vicious war of attrition and Johnson found himself the subject of bitter castigation by the antiwar movement, frequently facing shouts of "Hey, hey, L.B.J., how many kids did you kill today?"

Despite his unpopularity, Johnson still believed that he could be reelected in 1968—that is, until he won only a narrow victory in the New Hampshire presidential primary. To universal surprise, the demoralized Johnson withdrew from the race and retired to Texas, where he died in 1973—a day before a ceasefire halted the Vietnam War.

Lyndon B. Johnson stepped into Kennedy's shoes but was elected in his own right in 1964.

Lyndon Baines Johnson, the 36th president of the United States. Johnson was sworn in as U.S. president only hours after the assassination of John F. Kennedy, on the presidential jet *Air Force One.*

President Lyndon B. Johnson confers with Richard Nixon prior to the ceremonies of Nixon's Inauguration Day on January 20, 1969.

President Richard Nixon pictured at Otopeni Airport, near Bucharest, with Romanian dictator Nicolae Ceausescu.

Left: Richard Nixon, pictured while serving as Eisenhower's vice president, with his wife Pat.

38.

GERALD R. FORD (b.1913)

Republican. President 1974–1977

Vice president: Nelson A. Rockefeller

Gerald Ford was the only president of the United States to be sworn in as a result of the previous incumbent's resignation. Although he was never elected in his own right—either as president, or as vice president—he performed a valuable service in helping to restore the shattered public confidence in the United States' highest executive office.

Two years after Leslie King, Jr.'s birth in 1913, in Omaha, Nebraska, his parents divorced and Ford took his stepfather's name—Gerald Rudolph Ford—and moved to Grand Rapids, Michigan. He attended the University of Michigan between 1931 and 1935, graduating in economics and political science. At Michigan he had been an outstanding football player, and his sporting prowess resulted in a position as assistant football and boxing coach at Yale University, where he also studied law. Having obtained his law degree and admission to the bar in 1941, Ford practiced law until World War II interrupted his career. Between 1941 and 1945 he served in the navy, after which the lieutenant commander returned to his legal practice.

His election to the U.S. House of Representatives in 1948 began 25 years of continuous service in Congress, eight of which (between 1965 and 1973) were spent as Republican minority leader. As a congressman Ford generally faithfully supported conservative Republican policies. The affable and dutiful Ford might have remained in Congress had not Nixon asked him to replace Vice President Spiro Agnew in 1973, following the latter's resignation over an uncontested criminal charge for tax evasion. Following Congress's approval of his appointment Ford served as Nixon's loyal vice president right up to the president's own resignation in the face of impeachment over the Watergate scandal in August 1974.

President Ford pardoned Nixon a month later, but was not highly regarded for doing so.

The new president was initially confronted with the pressing, but difficult, task of restoring the nation's trust in the executive branch of government; this he eventually managed by means of his reform of the F.B.I. and C.I.A., and by his replacement of all but three members of Nixon's cabinet. His personal integrity and manifest honesty (if not his intellectual brilliance), were further instrumental in rehabilitating the presidency. At home he fought the inflation and recession that was afflicting the United States by initiating the cautious, conservative "W.I.N." ("Whip Inflation Now") program, with some success, although unemployment and inflation remained high.

In his foreign program, Ford continued Nixon's policy of *détente* with the Soviet Union, and after the collapse of South Vietnam in 1975 finally ordered the remaining U.S. troops in Vietnam home. Perhaps the most dramatic crisis of Ford's presidency was the Mayaguez incident in 1975, when he authorized U.S. military forces to free an U.S. cargo ship that had been seized by Cambodia's hostile Khmer Rouge. In addition, in 1975 Ford helped to stabilize the volatile situation in the Middle East by means of an Israeli-Egyptian pact that was mediated by Kissinger.

Despite his efforts in confidence-building following Watergate, which resulted in his nomination as Republican presidential candidate over Ronald Reagan, Ford was narrowly defeated by the Democrat Jimmy Carter in the presidential election of 1976. Given the profound damage caused to the Republican reputation during Watergate, this was, perhaps inevitable. Ford continues to enjoy an active retirement, although his name has to some extent been eclipsed by that of his wife, the founder of the Betty Ford addiction-rehabilitation clinic.

President Gerald R. Ford concedes defeat to Jimmy Carter at the White House in 1976.

39.

JIMMY CARTER (b.1924)

Democrat. President 1977–1981

Vice president: Walter F. Mondale

Despite Ford's best efforts, Jimmy Carter was elected the 39th president of the United States in 1976 in reflection of the public's desire to have a fresh, Democratic start after the largely discredited years of Republicanism. Despite his idealism and enthusiasm, however, Carter's term in office ended in humiliation.

Carter was born in 1924 in Plains, Georgia, into a middle-class farming family. After attending Georgia Southwestern College he was appointed to the United States Naval Academy at Annapolis and graduated in 1946. During his naval career Carter served on a battleship and submarine, studied nuclear physics at Union College, Schenectady, and became a nuclear-submarine engineer. However, he resigned from the navy and returned to Plains on the death of his father in 1953, thereafter managing and increasing the family's interests, which included a peanut farm. His interest in politics flourished—largely as a result of his opposition to segregation—and in 1962 he was voted as a Democrat to the Georgia senate, where he would serve two terms. Having failed to be elected governor of Georgia in 1966, Carter was successful on his second attempt in 1970 and earned a reputation as a liberal and progressive "New South" governor.

Ineligible to run for a second term as governor, Carter's subsequent decision to stand in the 1976 presidential election came as a surprise to most, and few rated his chances highly. After his defeat of ten rivals within the Democratic Party, however, Carter duly received the Democratic nomination, and went on to beat President Ford on a platform of openness, liberalism, and economic recovery. It had been a meteoric rise to power.

Carter was determined to signal his complete dissociation with the policies of the Republican regime, and his first act as president was the controversial pardoning of all draft evaders during the Vietnam War. The delicate economic situation that he had inherited from Ford worsened in 1978, and Carter attracted increasing censure in 1979, when inflation, oil shortages, and unemployment rose to new heights. Furthermore, many of his proposals, such as those intended to create an energy department, to reorganize the government, and to ratify the S.A.L.T. II treaty with the U.S.S.R., were opposed by both the Senate and the House of Representatives.

Running in parallel with his domestic problems were the crises that Carter faced in his foreign policy. An idealistic critic of the violation of human rights worldwide, like his predecessors Carter worked hard to reduce the tensions of the Cold War, but despite the restoration of diplomatic ties with China, the invasion of Afghanistan by the U.S.S.R in 1979 appeared to have negated his efforts. He did, however, score a notable triumph when Anwar Sadat of Egypt and Menachem Begin of Israel signed a peace treaty in 1978, following an intensive session of talks hosted by Carter at Camp David. In 1979 he faced a further, more dangerous, challenge, when the U.S. embassy in Teheran was seized by Iranian Shiite revolutionaries. Frustrated by his inability to resolve the situation by negotiation, and determined to secure the release of the 53 American hostages, Carter authorized a doomed rescue operation in 1980, with the loss of eight American lives.

Carter's popularity was now at an all-time low, and amid accusations of incompetence he lost the presidential election of 1980 to the Republican Ronald Reagan. On the day of Reagan's inauguration the hostages were released, and so it was Reagan who was credited, not Carter. Carter retired to Plains, where he remains a strong activist for human rights.

The Democratic politician and the 39th president of the United States of America, Jimmy Carter.

40.

RONALD W. REAGAN (b.1911)

Republican. President 1981–1989

Vice president: George H. W. Bush

Ronald Reagan may have been the U.S.A.'s oldest president to date, but he was also one of the most vigorous. His strongly nationalistic leadership, as well as his enthusiastic promotion of old-fashioned values and radical-conservative fiscal policies, made him a hero of the right and—along with British Prime Minister Margaret Thatcher—a symbol of the boom years of the 1980s.

Reagan was born in Tampico, Illinois, in 1911. At Eureka College, near Peoria, he studied economics and developed an interest in amateur theatricals; after graduation, in 1932 he became a radio sports announcer. Five years later, he traveled to Hollywood in search of fame and fortune, thus beginning a 27-year-long career as an actor, during which he appeared in over 50 mediocre movies. Reagan became active in politics during the 1940s; although initially a "New Deal" Democrat, when, in 1947, he was voted president of the Screen Actors Guild (an A.F.L labor union), he displayed marked conservative tendencies by informing on suspected communists in the movie industry. By the 1950s Reagan's movie career was in decline, and in 1954 he was hired by General Electric as a public-relations representative; as such, he made numerous promotional television appearances.

In 1962 Reagan switched his allegiance to the Republican Party and soon became a spokesman for the party's conservative faction. A sensational, televized speech in 1964 in support of the Republican presidential candidate Barry Goldwater brought him to the notice of the Californian Republicans and resulted in his election as governor of California in 1966. During his eight-year period as governor Reagan put his conservative policies into practice, cutting taxes and welfare support in an attempt to reduce the state's spending. Following his failure to be nominated as such in 1968, Reagan was voted a Republican presidential candidate in 1976, but was marginally defeated by Ford. He would not suffer the same fate in 1980, and his promise of national renewal, his genial manner, and his familiar, photogenic features, all contributed to a landslide victory over Carter.

When, on the day of the 40th president's inauguration, the Iranian-embassy hostages were released it seemed a symbolic affirmation of the nation's endorsement of Reagan and he accordingly set to work to transform the U.S.A. By 1984, such was "the great communicator's" perceived success on all fronts that he received an unprecedented 525 electoral votes in the presidential election, banishing the Democrat Walter F. Mondale to obscurity. "Reaganomics" promoted deregulation, reduced taxes, supported big business and the military, and neglected social-welfare programs. Although these policies indeed helped to stimulate the economy, increased productivity, and reduced inflation and unemployment, trade and budget deficits increased, and the less affluent suffered.

In his foreign policy Reagan adopted an aggressively nationalistic stance, which, after the years of Carter's liberalism, restored U.S. pride. In 1983 he ordered the invasion of pro-Cuban Grenada and, in 1986, the bombing of Libya in retribution for Libya's support of anti-U.S. terrorists. Under Reagan the Strategic Defense Initiative ("Star Wars"), a program intended to intercept enemy missiles in space, came into being, as a result of which U.S.-Soviet relations suffered.

Right up to his retirement in 1989 Reagan remained hugely popular, his cozy charisma even enabling him to emerge from the Iran-Contra scandal of 1986 (in which profits from sales of weapons to Iran were used to fund "Contra" rebels in Nicaragua) relatively unscathed. At the time of the presidential election of 1988, however, Reagan was 77. He retired to California, where he currently lives with his wife Nancy.

Ronald Wilson Reagan, the 40th president of the United States. A former actor and president of the Screen Actors Guild, he was elected governor of California in 1966 and U.S. president in 1981.

41.

GEORGE H. W. BUSH (b.1924)

Republican. President 1989–1993

Vice president: J. Danforth Quayle

As vice president during the Reagan years, George Bush's election as 41st president of the United States can be largely regarded as a public mandate for the continuation of his popular predecessor's policies. Eclipsed by the personal charisma of Reagan, Bush's own leadership qualities would finally gain recognition during the war in the Persian Gulf of 1991, but would fail to secure his reelection.

Born in 1924, in Milton, Massachusetts, Bush later moved with his family to Greenwich, Connecticut. Both Bush's parents came from wealthy backgrounds, and his father furthermore served as a Republican U.S. senator between 1952 and 1963. Bush graduated from Phillips Academy in Massachusetts in 1942, whereupon he joined the navy and became the United States' youngest torpedo-bomber pilot during World War II. He was decorated for heroism after being shot down and subsequently rescued in the Pacific.

On his return to the United States in 1945 Bush resumed his studies at Yale University, where he majored in economics, graduating in 1948. He then moved to Texas, where he cofounded the Zapata Petroleum Corporation in 1953, was appointed president of the Zapata Offshore Company in 1954, and thus became a successful independent oilman. The first indication of his political ambition came in 1964, when he failed to be voted to the U.S. Senate; in 1966, however, he was elected to the U.S. House of Representatives as a Republican. He was reelected in 1968, but not in 1970. Thereafter, successive Republican presidents appointed Bush ambassador to the United Nations (1971–1973), chairman of the Republican National Committee (1973–1974), ambassador to China (1974–1975), and director of the C.I.A (1976–1977)—all positions in which he displayed his competence.

In 1980, having had his own hopes of being nominated the Republican presidential candidate dashed, Bush was chosen as Reagan's vice president. After the Reagan–Bush victory, Bush retained his position during both of Reagan's administrations, demonstrating a remarkably hands-on approach. When Reagan was shot in 1981 it was left to Bush to govern, and he was also responsible for the development of many fiscal measures, as well as a program for the suppression of drugs.

In 1988 Reagan was set for retirement and his loyal vice president was seen as a natural successor. Following an aggressive campaign, during which the infamous promise (broken in 1990) "Read my lips: No new taxes" was uttered, Bush scored a notable victory over the Democratic candidate, Michael Dukakis, and became the U.S.A.'s chief executive.

In his avowed intention of continuing Reagan's conservative domestic policies, while simultaneously attempting (and failing) to reduce the budget deficit, Bush found himself blocked by Congress, for Democrats controlled both the House of Representatives and the Senate. Moreover, by 1990 the U.S. economy was in recession.

Then, when Saddam Hussein's Iraqi forces invaded Kuwait in 1990, Bush seized the opportunity both to prove himself and to divert attention from his unpopular domestic policies. Leading an international political and military coalition, Bush secured the defeat of Iraq by means of a short, but decisive, war in the Persian Gulf. It had been a calculated gamble: the horrors of Vietnam had hardened public opinion against any involvement in a "foreign" war, but Bush hoped that the coalition victory would strengthen his position at home. Not enough, apparently: by the time of the presidential election of 1992 the Republican Party was divided and the U.S. public disenchanted with Bush's right-wing fiscal and social policies. As a result, the Democrat Bill Clinton was elected the U.S.A.'s 42nd president.

George Herbert Walker Bush, the 41st president of the United States.
He held such positions as ambassador to the U.N. and director of the C.I.A. before his presidency.

42.

BILL CLINTON (b. 1946)

Democrat. President 1993–2000

Vice president: Albert Gore

During the presidential election of 1992 Bill Clinton unashamedly allowed comparisons to be drawn between himself and Kennedy, no doubt hoping that some of the glamor and mystique of "Camelot" would rub off on him. His presidency was, however, dogged by allegations of sexual harassment, his alleged involvement in the Whitewater affair, and his affair with the White House intern Monica Lewinsky.

William Jefferson Blythe IV was born in 1946, in Hope, Arkansas. His father died shortly before his birth and after his mother's remarriage her son took his stepfather's surname: Clinton. Clinton met Kennedy briefly in 1963 and later claimed the former president as his role model. The encounter certainly inflamed his interest in politics, and after he left Arkansas in 1964 to study at Georgetown University in Washington, D.C., Clinton worked in Senator Fulbright's office. Following his graduation in 1968 Clinton won a Rhodes scholarship and studied at Oxford University in England for two years. He subsequently returned to the United States to attend Yale University Law School, and was awarded a degree in 1973.

Back in Arkansas, in 1974 Clinton failed to be elected a Democratic congressman. He was instead elected attorney general of Arkansas in 1976, and, in 1978, governor—the youngest in the United States. Despite his failure to be reelected in 1980 (due to public dissatisfaction with his radical policies), Clinton regained the governorship in 1982 on a more moderate platform; "Slick Willie" remained in this position until his election as president. During his decade as governor, Clinton implemented a strong Democratic program that included tax increases and job creation schemes. He also cultivated national contacts and served as chairman of the National Governors' Association in 1986 and 1987, as well as of the Democratic Leadership Council in 1990 and 1991.

Surviving allegations of draft-dodging, extramarital affairs, and drug abuse, in 1992 Clinton secured the Democratic nomination for the presidency. During the subsequent election he stressed his youth, his moderate Democratic views, and his determination to work for the disadvantaged. Bush fought back by condemning Clinton as a "tax-and-spend liberal," but not even the entry of the independent candidate Ross Perot into the race could prevent Clinton's eventual victory.

Clinton had little success in his domestic policies. He appointed his wife, Hillary Rodham Clinton, to head a task force to reform health care, but in 1994 the Senate obstructed a vote on the modified program; in 1993, however, Congress did ratify the North American Free Trade Agreement (N.A.F.T.A). The Republicans gained control of both the Senate and Congress in 1994, thus forcing Clinton to compromise on most of his measures—including tax cuts and the reform of the welfare system—simultaneously alienating many Democrats. In his foreign policy Clinton proved himself a more credible leader: by threatening to invade Haiti in 1994, for example, he enabled a peaceful U.S. occupation of the country. He seemed to have attained a statesmanlike status by means of his brokerage of agreements between the P.L.O and Israel, as well as the combatants in Bosnia-Herzegovnia, and helped obtain a short-lived I.R.A. ceasefire.

Reelected in 1996, Clinton pursued a vigorous foreign policy during his second term, continuing to push for peace in Northern Ireland, as well as sending U.S. bombers to Iraq and troops to Kosovo. His second term was blighted by the revelation of his affair with Lewinsky, however, especially when he was proved to have lied. Although he avoided impeachment, his reputation was irreparably damaged.

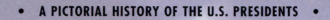

President Bill Clinton, who narrowly avoided impeachment following the Monica Lewinsky scandal.

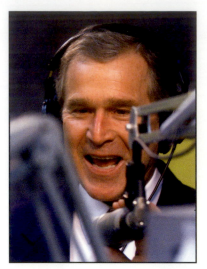

43.

GEORGE W. BUSH (b. 1946)

Republican President 2001–

Vice president: Richard B. Cheney

Bush became the 43rd president after an almost unprecedented series of events that saw him finally claiming victory after almost 40 days of legal action.

The scion of a formidable political dynasty: the grandson of a senator, the son of the 41st president of the United States, and the brother of the governor of Florida, all of them Republicans, Bush was born in New Haven, Connecticut, in 1946, then moved with his family to Texas in 1953, where his father, George H. W. Bush, carved out a successful career in the oil industry before entering politics in 1966. Like his father before him, Bush was educated at Yale University, graduating in 1968. He joined the Texas Air National Guard in the same year, working as a pilot until 1973.

Armed with an M.B.A. from Harvard Business School, in 1975 Bush set up the Bush Exploration Oil and Gas Company in Midland, Texas, which he presided over until 1986. In 1989, in conjunction with a number of associates, he acquired the franchise for the Texas Rangers baseball team, acting as its managing general partner until 1994, when the allure of a political career became too strong. He failed to win the Republican Party's nomination for a seat in the U.S. Congress in his first attempt in 1978, and it was not until 1994 that he gained public office, when he was voted governor of Texas, being reelected in 1998.

During his gubernatorial period, he focused primarily on the dual goals of improving educational facilities for children, and encouraging the citizens of Texas to help themselves by limiting governmental intervention and promoting entrepreneurship. His tough position on law and order saw Texas have the highest number of executions of prisoners on death row of all the United States. During the battle for the Republican nomination for president, the popularity of Bush's politics of "compassionate conservatism," as well as his spectacular fundraising ability, resulted in the defeat of his leading challenger, John McCain, in March 2000. In an attempt to parry any accusations of inexperience, Bush chose Dick Cheney as his vice-presidential running mate. Cheney had served as U.S. Defense Secretary in his father's administration.

During the mudslinging that is an inevitable feature of any political campaign, not only was Bush accused of various youthful misdemeanors, but also of arrogantly trading on his father's wealth and political record. He successfully countered these charges, however, with his convincing portrayal of a self-made businessman, popular governor, down-to-earth Texan, devout Methodist, and wholesome family man. Rather more damaging, however, was the perception that he lacked gravitas, an impression reinforced by some unfortunate media appearances, unguarded words, and muddled syntax, such "Bushisms" being gleefully seized upon by the media and Democrats alike.

Against his Democrat opponent, Albert Gore, Bush lost the popular vote, and gained the electoral advantage in Florida that got him the presidency only after ballot recounts and legal wrangling that went as far as the U.S. Supreme Court.

U.S. States, Including Date of Joining Union
(in chronological order)

Delaware	1787	Michigan	1837
New Jersey	1787	Florida	1845
Pennsylvania	1787	Texas	1845
Connecticut	1788	Iowa	1846
Georgia	1788	Wisconsin	1848
Maryland	1788	California	1850
Massachusetts	1788	Minnesota	1858
New Hampshire	1788	Oregon	1859
New York	1788	Kansas	1861
South Carolina	1788	West Virginia	1863
Virginia	1788	Nevada	1864
North Carolina	1789	Nebraska	1867
Rhode Island	1790	Colorado	1876
D.C.	1790–91	Montana	1889
Vermont	1791	North Dakota	1889
Kentucky	1792	South Dakota	1889
Tennessee	1796	Washington	1889
Ohio	1803	Idaho	1890
Louisiana	1812	Wyoming	1890
Indiana	1816	Utah	1896
Mississippi	1817	Oklahoma	1907
Illinois	1818	Arizona	1912
Alabama	1819	New Mexico	1912
Maine	1820	Alaska	1959
Missouri	1821	Hawaii	1959
Arkansas	1836		

= 50 states + District of Columbia

U.S. Presidents
Voting Results: Electoral College, Popular Votes, States

(E) = Electoral College vote
(P) = Popular vote

1789 George Washington

George Washington..69 (E)
John Adams...34 (E)
John Jay ....9 (E)
Others ....26 (E)
Not voted...12 (E)
[11 states]

1792 George Washington, Federalist, reelected

George Washington, Federalist.....................132 (E)
John Adams, Federalist ....77 (E)
George Clinton, Democratic-Republican......50 (E)
Thomas Jefferson ....4 (E)
Aaron Burr ....1 (E)
[15 states]

1796 John Adams, Federalist

John Adams, Federalist ....71 (E)
Thomas Jefferson, Democratic-Republican ...68 (E)
Thomas Pinckney, Federalist ....59 (E)
Aaron Burr, Anti-Federalist ....30 (E)
Samuel Adams, Democratic-Republican........15 (E)
Oliver Ellsworth, Federalist ....11 (E)
George Clinton, Democratic-Republican ....7 (E)
John Jay, Independent-Federalist.....................5 (E)
James Iredell, Federalist ....3 (E)
George Washington, Federalist........................2 (E)
John Henry, Independent................................2 (E)
S. Johnston, Independent-Federalist................2 (E)
Charles C. Pinckney, Independent-Federalist ...1 (E)
[16 states]

1800 Thomas Jefferson, Democratic Republican

Thomas Jefferson, Democratic-Republican ...73 (E)
Aaron Burr, Democrat-Republican ....73 (E)

John Adams, Federalist ....65 (E)
Charles C. Pinckney, Federalist. ....64 (E)
John Jay, Federalist..1 (E)
[16 states]
Jefferson: New York, Virginia, Kentucky,
      Tennessee, Georgia, South Carolina
Burr: Massachusetts, New Hampshire,
      Vermont, Rhode Island, Connecticut,
      New Jersey, Delaware
Split: Pennsylvania, North Carolina, Maryland

1804 Thomas Jefferson, Democratic-Republican, reelected

Thomas Jefferson, Democratic-Republican .162 (E)
Charles C. Pinckney, Federalist......................14 (E)
[17 states]
Jefferson: all states + Ohio except:
Pinckney: Connecticut, Delaware
Split: Maryland

John Adams

James Monroe

1808 James Madison, Democratic-Republican

4

James Madison, Democratic-Republican ....122 (E)
Charles C. Pinckney, Federalist ....47 (E)
George Clinton, Independent-Republican ....6 (E)
Not voted ....1 (E)
[17 states]
Madison: all states except:
Pinckney: Massachusetts, New Hampshire,
    Connecticut, Rhode Island, Delaware
Split: Madison/Pinckney/Clinton: Maryland,
    New York, North Carolina

1812 James Madison, Democratic-Republican, reelected

James Madison, Democratic-Republican ....128 (E)
De Witt Clinton, Fusion .... 89 (E)
Not voted ....1 (E)
[18 states]
Madison: all states + Louisiana except:
Clinton: Massachusetts, New York,
    New Hampshire, Connecticut, Rhode Island,
    New Jersey, Delaware
Split: Maryland

1816 James Monroe, Republican

5

James Monroe, Republican ....183 (E)
Rufus King, Federalist ....34 (E)
Not voted ....4 (E)
[19 states]
Monroe: all states + Indiana except:
    King: Massachusetts, Connecticut, Delaware

1820 James Monroe, Republican, reelected

James Monroe, Republican ....231 (E)
John Quincy Adams, Independent-Republican ....1 (E)
Not voted ....3 (E)
[24 states]
Monroe: all states + Maine, Illinois, Missouri,
    Mississippi, Alabama except:
Split: New Hampshire

1824 John Quincy Adams, Democratic-Republican

6

John Quincy Adams, Democratic-Republican ....
....84 (E), 108,740 (P)
Andrew Jackson, Democratic-Republican ....
....99 (E), 153,544 (P)
Henry Clay, Democratic-Republican ....
....37 (E), 47,136 (P)
William H. Crawford, Democratic-Republican ....
....41 (E), 46,618 (P)
[24 states]
Adams: all states except:
Jackson: Indiana, Pennsylvania, New Jersey,
    Missouri, Alabama, South Carolina, North
    Carolina, Tennessee
Clay: Missouri, Kentucky, Ohio
Crawford: Georgia, Virginia
Split: Illinois, Louisiana, Maryland, Delaware,
    New York

1828 Andrew Jackson, Democrat

7

Andrew Jackson, Democrat ....178 (E), 647,286 (P)
John Quincy Adams, National Republican ....
....83 (E), 508,064 (P)
[24 states]
Jackson: all states except:
Adams: New Hampshire, Vermont,
    Massachusetts, Connecticut, Rhode Island,
    New Jersey, Delaware
Split: Maine, New York, Maryland

1832 Andrew Jackson, Democrat, reelected

Andrew Jackson, Democrat......219 (E), 687,502 (P)
Henry Clay, National Republican.............................
....49 (E), 530,189 (P)
William Wirt, Anti-Masonic.....................7 (E), 0 (P)
John Floyd, Nullifiers.............................11 (E), 0 (P)
Not voted...2 (E)
[24 states]
Jackson: all states except:
Clay: Massachusetts, Connecticut,
    Rhode Island, Delaware, Kentucky
Wirt: Vermont
Floyd: South Carolina
Split: Maryland

1836 Martin Van Buren, Democrat

8

Martin Van Buren, Democrat......170 (E), 765,483 (P)
William Henry Harrison, Whig.......73 (E), shared (P)
Hugh L. White, Whig ....26 (E), shared (P) 739,795
Daniel Webster, Whig.......................14 (E), shared (P)
W. P. Mangum, Anti-Jackson ....11 (E), 0 (P)
[26 states]
Van Buren: all states + Arkansas, Michigan
Harrison: Indiana, Ohio, Kentucky, Vermont,
    Maryland, Delaware, New Jersey
White: Georgia, Tennessee
Webster: Massachusetts
Mangum: South Carolina

1840 William Henry Harrison, Whig

9

William Henry Harrison, Whig...234 (E), 1,274,624 (P)
Martin Van Buren, Democrat........60 (E), 1,127,781 (P)
[26 states]
Harrison: All states, except:
Van Buren: Arkansas, Missouri, Illinois, Alabama,
    South Carolina, Virginia, New Hampshire

1841 John Tyler, Whig

10

Became president in 1841 on the death of
Harrison—no election.

1844 James K. Polk, Democrat

11

James K. Polk, Democrat.........170 (E), 1,338,464 (P)
Henry Clay, Whig ....105 (E), 1,300,097 (P)
James G. Birney, Liberty...................0 (E), 62,300 (P)
[26 states]

Polk: all states except:
Clay: Tennessee, North Carolina, Kentucky, Ohio,
Maryland, Delaware, New Jersey, Connecticut,
    Rhode Island, Massachusetts, Vermont

1848 Zachary Taylor, Whig

Zachary Taylor, Whig...............163 (E), 1,360,967 (P)
Lewis Cass, Democrat..............127 (E), 1,222,342 (P)
Martin Van Buren, Free Soil ....0 (E), 291,263 (P)
[30 states]
Taylor: all states + Florida, except:
Cass: Texas, Iowa, Wisconsin, Missouri, Illinois,
    Arkansas, Indiana, Ohio, Michigan, Virginia,
    North Carolina, Alabama, Mississippi,
    New Hampshire, Maine

12

1850 Millard Fillmore, Whig

Became president in 1850 on death of Taylor—
no election.

13

Millard Fillmore

Franklin Pierce

1860 Abraham Lincoln, Republican

16

Abraham Lincoln, Republican.....180 (E), 1,865,593 (P)
John C. Breckinridge, Democrat...72 (E), 848,356 (P)
Stephen A. Douglas, Democrat....12 (E), 1,382,711 (P)
John Bell, Constitutional Union...39 (E), 592,906 (P)
[33 states]
Lincoln: all states + Oregon and Minnesota except:
Breckinridge: Texas, Louisiana, Arkansas,
    Mississippi, Alabama, Florida, South Carolina,
    North Carolina, Georgia, Maryland, Delaware
Douglas: Missouri
Bell: Kentucky, Tennessee, Virginia
Split: New Jersey

1864 Abraham Lincoln, Republican, reelected

Abraham Lincoln, Republican .....212 (E), 2,206,938 (P)
George B. McClellan, Democrat................................
....21 (E), 1,803,787 (P)
Not voted...81 (E), 0 (P)
[36 states]
Lincoln: all states + Nevada, Kansas, West
   Virginia except:
McClellan: Kentucky, Delaware, New Jersey

1865 Andrew Johnson, Democrat

17

Became president in 1865 on the assassination of
    Lincoln—no election.

1868 Ulysses S. Grant, Republican

18

Ulysses S. Grant, Republican ...214 (E), 3,013,421 (P)
Horatio Seymour, Democrat ......80 (E), 2,706,829 (P)
Not voted...23 (E), 0 (P)
[37 states]
Grant: all states + Nebraska except:
Seymour: Oregon, Louisiana, Georgia,
    Kentucky, Maryland, Delaware, New Jersey,
    New York

1852 Franklin Pierce, Democrat

14

Franklin Pierce, Democrat ....254 (E), 1,601,117 (P)
Winfield Scott, Whig................42 (E), 1,385,453 (P)
John P. Hale, Free Soil....................0 (E), 155,825 (P)
[31 states]
Pierce: all states + California except:
Scott: Kentucky, Tennessee, Vermont,
    Massachusetts

1856 James Buchanan, Democrat

15

James Buchanan, Democrat ....174 (E), 1,832,995 (P)
John C. Frémont, Republican..114 (E), 1,339,932 (P)
Millard Fillmore, Know-Nothing ...8 (E), 871,731 (P)
[31 states]
Buchanan: All states, except:
Frémont: Iowa, Wisconsin, Michigan, Ohio,
    New York, Vermont, New Hampshire, Maine,
    Massachusetts, Connecticut, Rhode Island
Fillmore: Maryland

1872 Ulysses S. Grant, Republican, reelected

Ulysses S. Grant, Republican ....286 (E), 3,596,745 (P)
Horace Greeley, Democrat..
[3 votes (E), but discounted on his death], 2,843,445 (P)
Charles O'Connor, Straight Democrat........................
....0 (E), 29,489 (P)
Thomas A. Hendricks, Independent Democrat ....
....42 (E), 0 (P)

B. Gratz Brown, Democrat ....18 (E), 0 (P)
Charles J. Jenkins, Democrat ....2 (E), 0 (P)
David Davis, Democrat............................1 (E), 0 (P)
Not voted...17 (E), 0 (P)
[37 states]
Grant: All states, except:
Hendricks: Texas, Maryland, Tennessee
Greeley: Georgia
Split: Missouri, Kentucky

1876 Rutherford B. Hayes, Republican

19

Rutherford B. Hayes, Republican ....
....185 (E), 4,036,572 (P)
Samuel J. Tilden, Democrat ....184 (E), 4,284,020 (P)
Peter Cooper, Greenback ....0 (E), 81,737 (P)
[38 states]
Hayes: all states + Colorado except:
Tilden: Texas, Missouri, Arkansas, Mississippi,
    Alabama, Georgia, Tennessee, North Carolina,
    Virginia, Kentucky, Indiana, West Virginia,
    Virginia, Maryland, Delaware, New
    Jersey, New York, Connecticut

1880 James A. Garfield, Republican

20

James A. Garfield, Republican.......214 (E), 4,453,295(P)
Winfield S. Hancock, Democrat .155 (E), 4,414,082 (P)
James B. Weaver, Greenback–Labor ......0 (E), 308,578(P)
Neal Dow, Prohibition.....................0 (E), 10,305 (P)
[38 states]
Garfield: all states except:
Hancock: Nevada, Texas, Missouri, Mississippi,
    Alabama, Georgia, Florida, South Carolina,
    North Carolina, Tennessee, Kentucky, Virginia,
    West Virginia, Maryland, Delaware, New Jersey
Split: California

1881 Chester A. Arthur, Republican

21

Became president in 1881 on the assassination of
Garfield—no election.

1884 Grover Cleveland, Democrat

22

Grover Cleveland, Democrat .....219 (E), 4,879,507 (P)
James G. Blaine, Republican ......182 (E), 4,850,293 (P)
Benjamin F. Butler, Greenback–Labor ....
....0 (E),175,370 (P)
John P. St. John, Prohibition ....0 (E), 150,369 (P)
[38 states]

Cleveland: all states except:
Blaine: Oregon, California, Nevada, Colorado,
    Nebraska, Kansas, Minnesota, Iowa,
    Wisconsin, Illinois, Michigan, Ohio,
    Pennsylvania, Vermont, New Hampshire,
    Maine, Massachusetts, Rhode Island

1888 Benjamin Harrison, Republican

23

Benjamin Harrison, Republican....233 (E), 5,447,129 (P)
Grover Cleveland, Democrat .....168 (E), 5,537,857 (P)
Clinton B. Fisk, Prohibition ....0 (E), 249,505 (P)
Anson J. Streeter, Union Labor.......0 (E), 146,935 (P)
[38 states]
Harrison: all states except:
Cleveland: Texas + Greer County, Missouri,
    Arkansas, Louisiana, Mississippi, Alabama,
    Georgia, Florida, South Carolina, North
    Carolina, Tennessee, Kentucky, West Virginia,
    Virginia, Maryland, Delaware, New Jersey,
    Connecticut

Benjamin Harrison

Grover Cleveland

1892 Grover Cleveland, Democrat

24

Grover Cleveland, Democrat......277 (E), 5,555,426 (P)
Benjamin Harrison, Republican....145 (E), 5,182,690 (P)
James B. Weaver, People's ....22 (E), 1,029,846 (P)
John Bidwell, Prohibition ....0 (E), 264,133 (P)
Simon Wing, Socialist Labor ....0 (E), 21,164 (P)
[44 states]
Cleveland: all states except:
Harrison: Washington, Montana, Wyoming,
    South Dakota, Nebraska, Minnesota, Iowa,
    Michigan, Pennsylvania, Vermont, New
    Hampshire, Maine, Massachusetts,
    Rhode Island
Weaver: Nevada, Idaho, Colorado, Kansas
Split: California, Oregon, North Dakota, Ohio

1896 William McKinley, Republican

25

William McKinley, Republican....271 (E), 7,102,246 (P)
William J. Bryan, Democrat......176 (E), 6,492,559 (P)
John M. Palmer, National Democrat ....
....0 (E), 133,148 (P)
Joshua Levering, Prohibition ....0 (E), 132,007 (P)
Charles H. Matchett, Socialist Labor .....0 (E), 36,274 (P)
Charles E. Bentley, Nationalist..........0 (E), 13,969 (P)
[45 states]
McKinley: all states except:
Bryan: Washington, Idaho, Nevada, Utah,
    Montana, Wyoming, Colorado, South Dakota,
    Nebraska, Kansas, Texas, Missouri, Arkansas,
    Louisiana, Mississippi, Alabama, Georgia,
    Florida, South Carolina, North Carolina,
    Tennessee, Virginia
Split: California, Kentucky

1900 William McKinley, Republican, reelected

William McKinley, Republican.....292 (E), 7,218,491 (P)
William J. Bryan, Democrat......155 (E), 6,356,734 (P)
John C. Wooley, Prohibition ....0 (E), 208,914 (P)
Eugene V. Debs, Socialist ....0 (E), 87,814 (P)
Wharton Baker, People's ....0 (E), 50,373 (P)
Joseph F. Malloney, Socialist Labor ....0 (E), 39,739 (P)
[45 states]
McKinley: all states except:
Bryan: Idaho, Nevada, Montana, Colorado,
    Texas, Missouri, Arkansas, Louisiana,
    Mississippi, Alabama, Georgia, Florida,
    North Carolina, South Carolina, Tennessee,
    Kentucky, Virginia

1901 Theodore Roosevelt, Republican

26

Became president in 1901 on the assassination of
McKinley—no election.

1904 Theodore Roosevelt, Republican

Theodore Roosevelt, Republican ....
....336 (E), 7,628,461 (P)
Alton B. Parker, Democrat.......140 (E), 5,084,223 (P)
Eugene V. Debs, Socialist ....0 (E), 402,283 (P)
Silas C. Swallow, Prohibition ....0 (E), 258,536 (P)
Thomas E. Watson, People's............0 (E), 117,183 (P)
Charles H. Corregan, Socialist Labor .....0 (E), 31,249 (P)
[45 states]

Roosevelt: all states except:
Parker: Texas, Arkansas, Louisiana, Mississippi,
Alabama, Georgia, Florida, South Carolina,
North Carolina, Tennessee, Kentucky,
Virginia, Maryland

1908 William H. Taft, Republican

27

William H. Taft, Republican ....321 (E), 7,675,320 (P)
William J. Bryan, Democrat.....162 (E), 6,412,294 (P)
Eugene V. Debs, Socialist ....0 (E), 420,793 (P)
Eugene W. Chafin, Prohibition ....0 (E), 253,840 (P)
Thomas L. Hisgen, Independence ....0 (E), 82,872 (P)
Thomas E. Watson, People's..............0 (E), 29,100 (P)
August Gillhaus, Socialist Labor ....0 (E), 14,021 (P)
[46 states]
Taft: all states except:
Bryan: Nevada, Texas, Oklahoma, Colorado,
Nebraska, Arkansas, Louisiana, Mississippi,
Alabama, Georgia, Florida, South Carolina,
North Carolina, Tennessee, Kentucky,
Virginia, Maryland

1912 Woodrow Wilson, Democrat

28

Woodrow Wilson, Democrat ....435 (E), 6,296,547 (P)
Theodore Roosevelt, Progressive ....88 (E), 4,118,571 (P)
William H. Taft, Republican........8 (E), 3,486,720 (P)
Eugene V. Debs, Socialist ....0 (E), 900,672 (P)
Eugene W. Chafin, Prohibition.......0 (E), 206,275 (P)
Arthur E. Reimer, Socialist Labor.....0 (E) 28,750 (P)
[48 states]
Wilson: all states + Arizona and New Mexico except:
Roosevelt: Washington, California, South Dakota,
Minnesota, Michigan, Pennsylvania
Taft: Utah, Vermont

1916 Woodrow Wilson, Democrat, reelected

Woodrow Wilson, Democrat ....277 (E), 9,127,695 (P)
Charles E. Hughes, Republican ....254 (E), 8,533,507 (P)
A. L. Benson, Socialist ....0 (E), 585,113 (P)
J. Frank Hanly, Prohibition.............0 (E), 220,506 (P)
Arthur E. Reimer, Socialist Labor ....0 (E), 13,403 (P)
[48 states]
Wilson: all states except:
Hughes: Oregon, Minnesota, Iowa, Wisconsin,
Illinois, Michigan, Indiana, Pennsylvania,
New York, Vermont, Maine, Massachusetts,
Rhode Island, Connecticut, New Jersey, Delaware
Split: West Virginia

1920 Warren G. Harding, Republican

29

Warren G. Harding, Republican ....
....404 (E), 16,143,407 (P)
James M. Cox, Democrat.........127 (E), 9,130,328 (P)
Eugene V. Debs, Socialist ....0 (E), 919,799 (P)
P. P. Christensen, Farmer–Labor............0 (E), 265,411
Aaron S. Watkins, Prohibition ....0 (E), 189,408 (P)
James E. Ferguson, American............0 (E), 48,000 (P)
W. W. Cox, Socialist Labor................0 (E), 31,715 (P)
[48 states]
Harding: All states except:
Cox: Texas, Arkansas, Louisiana, Mississippi,
Alabama, Georgia, Florida, South Carolina,
North Carolina, Kentucky, Virginia

1924 Calvin Coolidge, Republican

30

Calvin Coolidge, Republican.....382 (E), 15,718,211 (P)
John W. Davis, Democrat ....136 (E), 8,385,283 (P)
Robert M. LaFollette, Progressive ..13 (E), 4,831,289 (P)
Herman P. Faris, Prohibition ....0 (E), 57,520 (P)
Frank T. Johns, Socialist Labor ....0 (E), 36,428 (P)
William Z. Foster, Workers ....0 (E), 36,386 (P)
Gilbert O. Nations, American............0 (E), 23,967 (P)
[48 states]

Woodrow Wilson

Coolidge: all states except:

Davis: Texas, Oklahoma, Arkansas, Louisiana, Mississippi, Alabama, Georgia, Florida, South Carolina, North Carolina, Tennessee, Virginia

LaFollette: Wisconsin

1928 Herbert C. Hoover, Republican

31

Herbert C. Hoover, Republican...............................
....444 (E), 21,391,993 (P)
Alfred E. Smith, Democrat ....87 (E), 15,016,169
Norman Thomas, Socialist..............0 (E), 267,835 (P)
Verne L. Reynolds, Socialist Labor........0 (E), 21,603 (P)
William Z. Foster, Workers ....0 (E), 21,181 (P)
William F. Varney, Prohibition...........0 (E), 20,106 (P)
[48 states]

Hoover: all states except:

Smith: Arkansas, Louisiana, Mississippi, Alabama, Georgia, South Carolina, Massachusetts, Rhode Island

1932 Franklin D. Roosevelt, Democrat

32

Franklin D. Roosevelt, Democrat...............................
....472 (E), 22,809,638 (P)
Herbert C. Hoover, Republican....59 (E), 15,758,901 (P)
Norman Thomas, Socialist..............0 (E), 881,951 (P)
William Z. Foster, Communist ....0 (E), 102,785 (P)
William D. Upshaw, Prohibition ....0 (E), 81,869 (P)
Verne L. Reynolds, Socialist Labor.........0 (E), 33,276 (P)
William H. Harvey, Liberty ....0 (E), 53,425 (P)
[48 states]

Roosevelt: All states, except:

Hoover: Pennsylvania, Delaware, Connecticut, Vermont, New Hampshire, Maine

1936 Franklin D. Roosevelt, Democrat, reelected

Franklin D. Roosevelt, Democrat...............................
....523 (E), 27,752,869 (P)
Alfred M. Landon, Republican........8 (E), 16,674,665
William Lemke, Union ....0 (E), 882,479 (P)
Norman Thomas, Socialist..............0 (E), 187,720 (P)
Earl Browder, Communist................0 (E), 80,159 (P)
D. Leigh Colvin, Prohibition ....0 (E), 37,847 (P)
[48 states]

Roosevelt: all states except:

Landon: Maine and Vermont

1940 Franklin D. Roosevelt, Democrat, reelected

Franklin D. Roosevelt, Democrat...............................
....449 (E), 27,307,819 (P)
Wendell L. Wilkie, Republican......82 (E), 22,321,018 (P)
Norman Thomas, Socialist................0 (E), 99,557 (P)
Roger W. Babson, Prohibition ....0 (E), 57,812 (P)
Earl Browder, Communist................0 (E), 46,251 (P)
John W. Aiken, Socialist Labor ....0 (E), 14,892 (P)
[48 states]

Roosevelt: all states except:

Wilkie: North Dakota, South Dakota, Nebraska, Kansas, Colorado, Iowa, Michigan, Indiana, Vermont, Maine

1944 Franklin D. Roosevelt, Democrat, reelected

Franklin D. Roosevelt, Democrat...............................
....432 (E), 25,606,585 (P)
Thomas E. Dewey, Republican .....99 (E), 22,014,745 (P)
Norman Thomas, Socialist................0 (E), 80,518 (P)
Claude A. Watson, Prohibition..........0 (E), 74,758 (P)
Edward A. Teichert, Socialist Labor ....0 (E), 45,336 (P)
[48 states]

Roosevelt: all states except:

Dewey: Wyoming, Colorado, North Dakota, South Dakota, Nebraska, Kansas, Iowa, Wisconsin, Indiana, Ohio, Vermont, Maine

1945 Harry S. Truman, Democrat

Became president in 1945 on the death of Roosevelt—no election.

33

1948 Harry S. Truman, Democrat

Harry S. Truman, Democrat........303 (E), 24,105,812 (P)
Thomas E. Dewey, Republican....189 (E), 21,970,065 (P)
J. Strom Thurmond, States' Rights ....
....39 (E), 1,169,063 (P)
Henry A. Wallace, Progressive ......0 (E), 1,157,172 (P)
Norman Thomas, Socialist..............0 (E), 139,414 (P)
Claude A. Watson, Prohibition........0 (E), 103,224 (P)
Edward A. Teichert, Socialist Labor ....0 (E), 29,244 (P)
[48 states]

Truman: all states except:

Dewey: Oregon, North Dakota, South Dakota, Nebraska, Kansas, Michigan, Indiana, Maryland, Delaware, New Jersey, Pennsylvania, New York, Connecticut, Vermont, New Hampshire, Maine

Thurmond: Louisiana, Mississippi, Alabama, South Carolina

34. 1952 Dwight D. Eisenhower, Republican

34

Dwight D. Eisenhower, Republican ....
....442 (E), 33,936,234 (P)
Adlai E. Stevenson, Democrat ....89 (E), 27,314,992 (P)
Vincent Hallinan, Progressive ....0 (E), 140,023 (P)
Stuart Hamblen, Prohibition ....0 (E), 72,949 (P)
Eric Haas, Socialist Labor ....0 (E), 30,267 (P)
Darlington Hoopes, Socialist ....0 (E), 20,203 (P)
Douglas A. MacArthur, Constitution ...0 (E), 17,205 (P)
[48 states]
Eisenhower: all states except:
Stevenson: Arkansas, Louisiana, Mississippi,
    Alabama, Georgia, South Carolina,
    North Carolina, Kentucky, West Virginia

1956 Dwight D. Eisenhower, Republican, reelected

Dwight D. Eisenhower, Republican ....
....457 (E), 35,590,472 (P)
Adlai E. Stevenson, Democrat ......73 (E), 26,022,752 (P)
T. Coleman Andrews, States' Rights.....0 (E), 107,929 (P)
Eric Haas, Socialist Labor ....0 (E), 44,300 (P)
[48 states]
Eisenhower: all states except:
Stevenson: Missouri, Arkansas, Alabama, Georgia,
    South Carolina, North Carolina
Split: Mississippi

1960 John F. Kennedy, Democrat

35

John F. Kennedy, Democrat ......303 (E), 34,221,485 (P)
Richard M. Nixon, Republican ..219 (E), 34,108,684 (P)
Orval Faubus, National States' Rights ....
.....................................0 (E), 227,881 (P)
Eric Haas, Socialist Labor ....0 (E), 48,031 (P)
Rutherford B. Decker, Prohibition ...0 (E), 45,197 (P)
Farrell Dobbs, Socialist Workers ....0 (E), 39,692 (P)
[50 states]
Kennedy: all states + Hawaii except:
Nixon: Alaska, Washington, Oregon, California,
    Idaho, Utah, Arizona, Montana, Wyoming,
    Colorado, North Dakota, South Dakota,
    Nebraska, Kansas, Oklahoma, Iowa,
    Wisconsin, Tennessee, Kentucky, Virginia,
    Indiana, Ohio, Vermont, New Hampshire,
    Maine
Split: Mississippi, Alabama

1963 Lyndon B. Johnson, Democrat

36

Became president in 1963 on the assassination of
Kennedy—no election.

1964 Lyndon B. Johnson, Democrat

Lyndon B. Johnson, Democrat ....
....486 (E), 43,126,233 (P)
Barry M. Goldwater, Republican ....
....52 (E), 27,174,989 (P)
Eric Haas, Socialist Labor ....0 (E), 45,186 (P)
Clifton DeBerry, Socialist Workers ....0 (E), 32,705 (P)
Earle Harold Munn, Prohibition ......0 (E), 23,267 (P)
[51 states]
Johnson: all states + D.C., except:
Goldwater: Arizona, Louisiana, Mississippi,
    Alabama, Georgia, South Carolina

Lyndon Johnson

Richard Nixon

George S. McGovern, Democrat.............................
....17 (E), 29,168,110 (P)
John G. Schmitz, American Independent ....
....0 (E), 1,106,052 (P)
Benjamin Spock, People's.................0 (E), 79,484 (P)
Linda Jenness or Evelyn Reed, Socialist Workers........
....0 (E), 97,256 (P)
Louis Fisher, Socialist Labor ....0 (E), 53,814 (P)
Gus Hall, Communist ....0 (E), 25,595 (P)
[51 states]
Nixon: all states except:
McGovern: D.C., Massachusetts

1974 Gerald R. Ford, Republican

Became president in 1974 on the resignation of Nixon—no election.

38

1976 Jimmy Carter, Democrat

Jimmy Carter, Democrat..........297 (E), 40,825,248 (P)
Gerald R. Ford, Republican.......241 (E), 39,147,779 (P)
Eugene J. McCarthy, Independent.....0 (E), 680,390 (P)
Lester G. Maddox, American Independent ....
....0 (E), 168,264 (P)
[51 states]
Carter: all states except:
Ford: Alaska, Washington, Oregon, California,
     Nevada, Idaho, Utah, Arizona, New Mexico,
     Colorado, Wyoming, Montana, North Dakota,
     South Dakota, Nebraska, Kansas, Oklahoma,
     Iowa, Illinois, Indiana, Michigan, Virginia,
     New Jersey, Connecticut, Vermont,
     New Hampshire, Maine

39

1968 Richard M. Nixon, Republican

37

Richard M. Nixon, Republican ....
....301 (E), 31,770,237 (P)
Hubert H. Humphrey, Democrat ....
....191 (E), 31,270,533 (P)
George C. Wallace, American Independent ....
....46 (E), 9,906,141 (P)
Henning Blomen, Socialist Labor ....0 (E), 52,588 (P)
Dick Gregory, New ....0 (E), 47,097 (P)
Fred Halstead, Socialist Workers ....0 (E), 41,300 (P)
Eldridge Cleaver, Peace and Freedom ....0 (E), 36,385 (P)
[51 states]
Nixon: All states, except:
Humphrey: Washington, Texas, Minnesota, Iowa,
     Michigan, West Virginia, D.C., Maryland,
     Pennsylvania, New York, Maine, Massachusetts,
     Rhode Island, Connecticut, Hawaii
Wallace: Arkansas, Louisiana, Mississippi,
     Alabama, Georgia

1972 Richard M. Nixon, Republican, reelected

Richard M. Nixon, Republican...521 (E), 47,165,234 (P)

1980 Ronald Reagan, Republican

Ronald Reagan, Republican......489 (E), 43,899,248 (P)
Jimmy Carter, Democrat ....49 (E), 35,481,435 (P)
John B. Anderson, Independent ....0 (E), 5,719,437 (P)
Ed Clark, Libertarian......................0 (E), 920,859 (P)
Barry Commoner, Citizens ....0 (E), 230,377 (P)
Gus Hall, Communist ....0 (E), 43,871 (P)
Clifton DeBerry, Socialist Workers........0 (E), 40,105 (P)
Ellen McCormack, Right-to-Life ....0 (E), 32,319 (P)
[51 states]
Reagan: all states except:
Carter: Minnesota, Georgia, West Virginia, D.C.,
     Maryland, Rhode Island, Hawaii

40

1984 Ronald Reagan, Republican, reelected

Ronald Reagan, Republican ....525 (E), 54,450,603 (P)
Walter F. Mondale, Democrat.......13 (E), 37,573,671 (P)
David Bergland, Libertarian ....0 (E), 227,949 (P)
Lyndon Larouche, Independent Democrats................
....0 (E), 76,773 (P)
Sonia Johnson, Citizens ....0 (E), 72, 153 (P)
Bob Richards, Populist.....................0 (E), 62,371 (P)
Dennis Serrette, Independent Alliance ....
....0 (E), 47,209 (P)
Gus Hall, Communist ....0 (E), 35,561 (P)
Mel Mason, Socialist Workers...........0 (E), 24,687 (P)
[51 states]
Reagan: all states except:
Mondale: D. C., Minnesota

1988 George Bush, Republican

41

George Bush, Republican......426 (E), 48,138,478 (P)
Michael Dukakis, Democrat ......112 (E), 41,114,068 (P)
Ron Paul, Libertarian.....................0 (E), 409,412 (P)
Lenora Fulani, New Alliance ....0 (E), 21,430 (P)
David Duke, Populist ....0 (E), 44,135 (P)
Eugene J. McCarthy, Consumer ....0 (E), 30,074 (P)
James Griffin, American Independent ....
....0 (E), 26,053 (P)
Lyndon LaRouche, National Economic Recovery.....
....0 (E), 23,713 (P)
[51 states]
Bush: all states except:
Dukakis: Hawaii, Washington, Oregon,
        Minnesota, Iowa, Wisconsin, West Virginia,
        D.C., Rhode Island, Massachusetts, New York

1992 Bill Clinton, Democrat

42

Bill Clinton, Democrat..........370 (E), 43,728,375 (P)
George Bush, Republican......168 (E), 38,167,416 (P)
Ross Perot, Independent............0 (E), 19,237,247 (P)
[51 states]
Clinton: all states except:
Bush: Alaska, Idaho, Utah, Arizona, Wyoming,
        North Dakota, South Dakota, Nebraska,
        Kansas, Oklahoma, Texas, Mississippi,
        Alabama, Florida, South Carolina,
        North Carolina, Virginia, Indiana

1996 Bill Clinton, Democrat, Reelected

Bill Clinton, Democrat ....379 (E), 47,402, 357 (P)
Bob Dole, Republican...........159 (E), 39,198,755 (P)
Ross Perot, Independent ....0 (E), 8,085,402 (P)
[51 states]
Clinton: all states except:
Dole: Alabama, Alaska, Idaho, Utah, Wyoming,
        Colorado, North Dakota, South Dakota,
        Georgia, Nebraska, Kansas, Indiana, Mississippi,
        Montana, North Carolina, South Carolina,
        Oklahoma, Texas, Virginia

2001 George W. Bush, Republican

43

George W. Bush, Republican .271 (E), 49,820,518 (P)
Albert Gore, Democrat..........269 (E), 50,158,094 (P)
Ralph Nader, Independent............0 (E), 2,756,08 (P)
[51 states]
Bush: all states except:
Gore: California, Connecticut, Delaware, Hawaii,
        Illinois, Iowa, Maine, Maryland, Massachusetts,
        Michigan, Minnesota, New Jersey, New Mexico,
        New York, Oregon, Pennsylvania, Rhode Island,
        Vermont, Washington, Wisconsin, Dist. of Col.

George Bush

Index

Acknowledgements

© Joseph Sohm; ChromoSohm Inc./ CORBIS for front cover (behind) and page 2 (above and throughout book) and back cover (above);
Hulton Getty Picture Collection for front cover (above) and pages 8, 10, 11, 12, 13, 15, 16, 17, 18, 19, 20, 22, 23, 24, 25, 26, 27, 28, 29, 30, 32, 33, 34, 35, 36, 37, 38, 39, 40, 41, 42, 43, 44, 45, 47, 48, 49, 50, 51, 52, 53, 54, 55, 56, 58, 60, 61, 62, 63, 64, 65, 66, 67, 68, 69, 70, 71, 72, 74, 75, 76, 77, 78, 80, 81, 84, 86, 87, 90, 91, 92, 96, 98, 100, 102, 103, 104 (Gary Franklin), 107, 108, 109, 110, 111, 112 (Ron Sachs/Consolidated News), 117, 118, 119, 120, 121, 122, 123, 125 and 126;
© Reuters NewMedia, Inc./CORBIS for front cover (below) and pages 114, 115 and 127;
© Bill Ross/CORBIS for page 2 (below) and back cover (below);
© Richard T. Nowitz/CORBIS for page 9;
© CORBIS for page 21, 88, 94, 99 and 106;
© Bettmann/CORBIS for pages 31, 59, 73, 79, 85, 89, 93 and 95 (above);
© Galen Rowell/CORBIS for page 46;
© Medford Historical Society Collection/CORBIS for page 57;
© Hulton-Deutsch Collection/CORBIS for pages 82 and 97;
© Oscar White/CORBIS for page 83;
© Richard Cummins/CORBIS for pages 95 (below) and 101;
© Leif Skoogfors/CORBIS for page 105;
© Wally McNamee/CORBIS for page 113.